Ground Level Christianity

Where the Rubber Meets the Road

Janice Gravely

Ground Level Christianity
Copyright © 1999 by Janice Gravely
ALL RIGHTS RESERVED

Unless otherwise indicated, all Scripture references are from the New International Version of the Bible, © copyright 1973, 1978, 1984 by International Bible Society, Colorado Springs, Colorado. References marked KJV are from the Authorized King James Version of the Bible. References marked NKJ are from the New King James Version of the Bible, © copyright 1979, 1980, 1982 by Thomas Nelson, Inc., Nashville, Tennessee. References marked TLB are from The Living Bible, © copyright 1971 by Tyndale House Publishers, Inc., Wheaton, Illinois. References marked AMP are from the Amplified Bible, © copyright 1987 by the Zondervan Corporation and the Lockman Foundation, La Habra Foundation, California. Passages marked PHIL are from the *New Testament in Modern English* by J. B. Phillips, copyright © 1958, 1959, 1960 by the MacMillan Company, New York, New York. References marked NLT are from the New Living Translation, © copyright 1996 by Tyndale House Publishers, Inc., Wheaton, Illinois. References marked NAS are from the New American Standard Bible, © copyright 1960, 1962, 1963, 1968, 1971, 1972, 1973, 1977 by the Lockman Foundation, La Habra, California.

Fairmont Books is a ministry of The McDougal Foundation, Inc., a Maryland nonprofit corporation dedicated to spreading the Gospel of the Lord Jesus Christ to as many people as possible in the shortest time possible.

Published by:

Fairmont Books
P.O. Box 3595
Hagerstown, MD 21742-3595

ISBN 1-884369-85-5

Printed in the United States of America
For Worldwide Distribution

Acknowledgments

Without the help and encouragement of my dear family and all the people in these stories who enriched my life and taught me the principles of *Ground Level Christianity*, there would be no such book. The Edmund Gravely family consists of four children — Keen, Peyton (now in Heaven), Jane and Louise with their children. We grew up in the faith together, as you will see in their stories. Jane, Louise and Kim, Peyton's wife, read and improved the writing. Jane overcame the technical difficulties, and Keen used his twenty-six years of experience with *The New York Times* to help with the editing.

Without the expertise of Harold McDougal and his staff, *Ground Level Christianity* would not be in your hands now, dear reader. We all labored together for a book that would please God.

And I thank you, dear reader, who picked up this book. May God bless you with every spiritual blessing in Christ Jesus and help you to grow in grace and stature and in favor with God and man — just like Jesus.

Janice Gravely
Rocky Mount, NC

Contents

Introduction 7

1. Where the Rubber Meets the Road 9
2. Dreama Meets the Master 15
3. Now, About the Bible 24
4. The Bible Is Alive 26
5. Finding Guidance in the Bible 34
6. Finding Fruit on the Golf Course 38
7. "You Will Receive Power..." 43
8. "...When the Holy Spirit Comes On You" 50
9. Treading Through the Minefields 63
10. "But Deliver Us From Evil" 70
11. "Sad Hearts, Weep No More" 76
12. They Will Drive Out Demons 85
13. Cleaning House 94
14. High-Stakes Fasting 105
15. The Power of Forgiveness 111
16. Tithing 116
17. The Power of Persistence in Prayer 122
18. Healing Comes 127
19. "What Must I Do to Be Saved?" 143
20. Humility: Who Needs It? 152
21. Worship 155
22. The Devil Made Me Do It 163
23. Choosing to Be Like Christ 170

The Last Word 179

Appendix: A Brief Sketch of the Bible 181

Introduction

Perhaps some readers can remember when God miraculously brought down a wife who couldn't fly from six thousand feet in the air when her pilot husband slumped unconscious over the controls of their airplane. The story was carried on the local and national news over television, radio and newspapers. Later the *Reader's Digest* and *Guideposts* magazines featured the event as a miracle. There is no other explanation. God did it.

Equally dramatic is the story of the way the woman crawled, with a broken pelvis and four broken ribs, a punctured lung and internal injuries, across a frozen, plowed-up field, to a house more than two hundred yards away. She was empowered by the Word of God which says, *"I can do all things through Christ which strengthens me"* (Philippians 4:13, NKJ). I was that woman, and this is my experience with Christianity at the ground level.

People often ask me, "Janice, I would have died of fright. How could you keep up your faith?"

My answer often is, "Well, if things are not too hard for you, you don't need God. When things are impossible, then only God is big enough to handle them. Either I had faith in God to bring us through, or I would surely die. I chose to have faith."

Crawling was a way of life with me in the years leading up to the airplane accident. With the help of God I crawled through problems attending family life, rearing four children, through illnesses, accidents and community responsibilities. In the twenty years before the airplane crash, I had learned to trust God in everything on the ground level. Then, when I was caught alone and helpless without the knowledge and skill to pilot a plane and no radio assistance, I knew I could call on Him. Most of that story can be found in my book *Won't Somebody Help Me!*

We all crawl. As babies we crawl before we walk. As baby Christians we crawl as we learn to live the Christian life. This is a book of true stories of people who have discovered for themselves some principles of life "in the Christ lane." Watch these people enter the Christian life and learn how to understand the Bible and use it for guidance. Observe them as they experience the fruit and the gifts of the Holy Spirit, as they walk in divine healing, and as they clean house spiritually, forgive, fast, tithe and lead others to Christ.

After experiencing all these stories of people learning to walk "in the Christ lane," I hope you can say with King David in the Bible (as I do), *"I was young and now I am old, yet I have never seen the righteous forsaken ..."* (Psalm 37:25). Then you, too, can crawl, walk or fly, if necessary, using *Ground Level Christianity*.

Chapter 1

Where the Rubber Meets the Road

Did you know that you are an eternal being, that though you may die physically, the most important part of you will go on living forever and ever? No science text documents this, and no scientific evidence will prove it, but it is, nevertheless, true, and it is true for everyone — whether they believe it or not. The topic has attracted wide interest throughout history, and recently many people have described what it is like to seem to die, to see Heaven or Hell and return to tell about it.

One popular book carefully documents the death of a man who was bloodily beaten and left hanging to suffocate to death. His death was legally certified, and he was entombed in rock. Days later he was found alive. He did not personally write about his experience, but observers wrote down what they saw and what he said. What they recorded is now part of the Bible, and the man they saw return from days of death was Jesus. His return from death after three days is unique, and He is, therefore, the authority on what happens after death.

Everyone has a part of his being that keeps on living beyond his death, which Jesus called the soul. Everyone will live eternally somewhere. The question is what is that eternal destination? Jesus, the authority on eternity, says that the destination can be with God or totally apart from God. The Bible shows that we are the ones who choose to accept or deny God's invitation to eternal life with Him. People make their choices at the strangest times and in unlikely ways, as my grandson David did.

David is the youngest in a family of four brothers and

Ground Level Christianity

sisters. When everybody in the family tells David what to do, sometimes he gets tired of it. As a child he knows who's boss — his parents — so he has to do what they want. But when he hears too much from his older siblings, he sometimes retorts, "I don't have to do what you say. You're not the boss of me!"

David, eight, and his brother, Kent, fourteen, were visiting my daughter Jane and me in the mountains one summer. At bedtime we have a wind-down time to decompress from the day. One night as I was reading a story, I felt a nudge from the Holy Spirit to ask David if he'd like to ask Jesus into his heart that night. From his Christian family David knew what was involved in his answer.

He thought a minute and said he reckoned not.

I resumed reading. A little farther along in the story, I thought to bring the subject up again. "David, Jesus loves you. He wants to come into your heart and live His life through you. He can't be your Savior and Lord unless you ask Him. Don't you want to ask Him?"

In the silence, I sensed that God was right there with us. From the Bible we knew that it was God's will that all men *"be saved"* and *"come to the knowledge of the truth"* (1 Timothy 2:4, KJV), and that included young David. Before the waiting became awkward, David got up, went to his bedside, and knelt with his hands folded in prayer.

"Dear Jesus," he said in a firm, clear voice. "I'm tired of trying to be my own boss. Will you come in and be the Boss of me?"

His eight-year-old prayer stated David's complete surrender to the Lord, and it started his eternal life with God. Eternal life with God starts just that simply.

To have eternal life with God, we must first be born physically and then spiritually. Jesus called the second birth being "born again." That is what it really means to become a Christian.

Before we get to questions that might arise, let me tell you my own story. As you read it, remember that everyone's experience is unique — and sometimes dramatic.

Where the Rubber Meets the Road

Before I became a Christian, I didn't realize that I needed to become one. As a child I was taught that there was a God who ordered the universe and who answered my prayers, but I didn't know Him, and I didn't know anyone who did. Once I prayed to pass algebra and when I did, I thought God had helped me. Mostly we left each other alone, or so I thought. While I was a student at UCLA, college intellectualism left no room for church.

Marriage brought me to the Bible-belt South, where I joined the Methodist Church when our firstborn son was christened. Even though I sang in the choir and tried to "do the right thing," it wasn't long before I realized that as a displaced Californian married into a Southern tobacco family, I was growing more and more unhappy. I had always tried to be moral and altruistic. Wasn't that enough?

"The Right Thing"

Grandmother Gravely, whom we called "Mother 'G' ," discovered I had never actually joined the church, so she set about to fix that problem. She arranged for a baptismal and christening ceremony in her spacious, high-ceilinged Victorian home, where the minister and extended family gathered in her parlor. About fifteen aunts, uncles and cousins surrounded our toddler son Keen and me, as we knelt on the thick, soft Chinese rug.

When Dr. Hillman, the minister, baptized us, he asked, "Do you earnestly repent of your sins and accept Jesus Christ as your Savior?"

Obediently I said, "I do."

The prayer took longer — so long I counted the toes encircling us and memorized the oriental pattern of the rug. He read from the prayer book: "O merciful God, grant that all sinful affections may die in this, thy servant, and all things belonging to thy Spirit may live and grow in her. Grant that she may receive the fullness of thy grace, and ever remain in the number of thy faithful and beloved children, through Jesus Christ our Lord."

Ground Level Christianity

Obediently I said "Amen."

Afterward, Mother G served everyone ice cream, and it was done. But nothing changed. If I had any "sinful affections" — whatever they are — they didn't die, and if I received any "grace" — whatever that is — it didn't show. Was this all there was to being a Christian? I was trying live right, but Jesus was still as far away as before, and the Bible was still a closed book to me. It was as if I had said "I do" and "Amen" and nobody was listening. But God heard and set in motion circumstances that brought the two of us face to face.

For the next four and a half years I had three more babies, sang in the choir, read the Bible out of duty and habit, prayed rote prayers and got deeper into despair, while my husband of eight years was building his business career and maintaining his plus-two golf handicap. During the summers, the children and I stayed with my husband's mother — Mother Louise — while her husband and mine were away on the Georgia tobacco markets. In an effort to make me happier, one night she encouraged me to go to a party while she stayed with the children.

After the party, I tiptoed in very late. Keyed up but unsatisfied by the party gaiety, I crawled into bed with only the bedside lamp making a pool of light in the dark wood-paneled room. More out of habit than hope, I picked up the Bible to read a minute, wanting to take the edge off my misery. I was reading from the gospel of John.

Suddenly, light flooded the room. Jesus was there! One moment I was reading about Him on the pages of the Bible, and the next moment He was standing in my room! The brilliance of His person and white robes radiated light and love into my being. From the foot of the bed He looked at me with eyes of love.

As I lay there, overcome with awe, the Lord's personality impacted my being. I was hardly able to bear the power and weight of His presence.

He spoke with deep tenderness, "Janice, your sins are forgiven. Go and sin no more." His words both reassured and baffled me.

Where the Rubber Meets the Road

Sins! Nobody had ever spoken to me about my sins before — only in the general way of "sinful affections" — whatever they were. Then I looked into my soul and saw pride — loathsome, awful pride. It was like a pit of snakes down inside me. I drew back in horror, but I could not get away from it. It was in me.

"Oh, forgive me, Lord," I prayed. "I didn't know that was in there. Help me. I cannot help myself."

I was seeing with new eyes, spiritual eyes that Jesus had given me. The same eyes that saw this wonderful Being and knew it was Jesus now looked within and saw sin.

His gentle look reminded me that he had forgiven my sins even before I asked. All I could do was accept what He had given.

New and Clean

Suddenly everything was new. I was clean. What a joy to know that God loves me, that Jesus is real, that He was speaking to me and that I could know Him! Then He was gone.

In the pool of light from the reading lamp I re-read the Bible passage — Jesus' conversation with the woman at the well — hoping He would come back. He did not come back that night, but the memory never left. From then on I knew that, although I couldn't see Him, He was always with me.

The next morning I asked Mother Louise to help me understand the night's experience with Jesus, but she couldn't explain it anymore than I could. I asked others for help, too. Soon I became intimidated and kept my heart-changing encounter to myself. But the hunger to know Jesus better increased.

The formal pledge taken in Mother G's parlor became a reality to me: "I do earnestly repent of my sins and accept Jesus Christ as my Savior." I do! But working this out in real life was to become a life-long process.

That was the beginning of my eternal life with God. My acceptance of Jesus as my Savior is more real every day. Day by day He has been answering the minister's long-ago prayer

Ground Level Christianity

that all sinful affections die and that all things of the Spirit live and grow in me with the fullness of God's grace. That is how eternal life with God begins, and only after that event can we fully understand some basic realities about God and spiritual life.

Until the Spirit of God enters a life, that person is half-dead. The body, mind and will keep us going, but the spirit part of us is dead. The spirit is the part that distinguishes humans from every other living creature. When we use our minds and will to ask Jesus to be our Lord and Savior, we become wholly alive with God's Spirit in us forever.

Only in this life do we have the opportunity to choose eternal life with God. Each one chooses for himself. Just being born into a Christian home or being baptized into a certain church does not get us into Heaven. It's a personal transaction with God. It can happen at any age, but if we die first, it's too late.

Some people like my grandson David come to Jesus quite simply, like a child, and some come like me, by a stroke of revelation or circumstance. Some come quite carefully and logically, like Dreama, my friend I will introduce more fully in the next chapter.

This new birth is where life really begins, where we start truly to live, *Where the Rubber Meets the Road.*

Chapter 2

Dreama Meets the Master

My friend Dreama walked into my life the day she came through the kitchen door to clean house for me. She was working part time while she went to the local community college.

"Would you like some coffee?" I asked before she started working. Her hazel eyes crinkled over her broad smile as she nodded yes.

"Sit down, and let's get acquainted."

We sat in an, old-fashioned paneled kitchen, on comfortable chairs, at a large table. It put us both at ease. We touched on work and families, and before long the talk turned to spiritual things.

After she told me that she had always wanted to be a Christian, she grew defensive. "I've gone to churches on and off all my life," she protested. "I know there is something there for people, but I've never found it. There's a church on every corner, but I don't know how to get in or who to ask what to do!"

"If you are talking about how to get into God's Kingdom, Dreama, that's His job. God loves you, and He wants you 'in' more than you want in. He's drawing you to Himself right now.

"The minute you ask Jesus to be your Lord and Savior, and believe in your heart that God raised Him from the dead, you'll be saved. Do you believe that God raised Jesus from the dead?" I asked.

"Of course. Doesn't everybody?" she replied.

"Well I do, and history documents it. So do you want Jesus to be your Savior and your Lord?"

"Of course. What do I have to do?"

Ground Level Christianity

"Just ask Him. Pray something like this: 'Dear Jesus, I believe You are the Son of God and that God raised You from the dead. Please come into my heart and be my Lord. I give the control of my life over to You. Please forgive me of my sins. Let me live for You in this life and with You in Heaven. In Your Name, Amen.'"

"I can't remember all that. Will you help me?"

So we prayed together. She did her part, and God did His. Dreama was instantly born again into the Kingdom of God in answer to her prayer. It reminded me of the words to the Christmas carol:

> *How silently, how silently the wondrous gift is given*
> *So God imparts to human hearts the wonders of his heaven.*[1]

Who cares about a little dust and dirt in the house when Jesus has just entered and swept this human heart clean? I didn't, so we kept on talking.

Dreama was full of questions. What had really happened to her, she asked?

"Well, Paul describes it as being delivered out of the power of darkness, and being translated into the kingdom of God's dear Son.[2] This is where the Christian life begins — the new birth," I explained.

"Why do we need to be delivered from the power of darkness?" she asked.

"Because we are descendants of Adam, and are born with his nature and characteristics — his rebellious, disobedient nature.

"It took me a long time to really believe that little babies are born with rebellion in their nature — that I was born with a rebellious disposition. Having babies and rearing children of my own, though, opened my eyes to that fact. I never had to teach them how to be disobedient or how to lie. I had to teach them how to obey and to tell the truth."

Dreama smiled ruefully over her coffee cup. With seven children of her own she identified with the problem.

Dreama Meets the Master

"Even after learning to 'be good,' we need a whole new nature. Like the one you received from Jesus just now. He replaced your Adamic nature with His own, and you became a child of God with a nature like His."

"What do you mean, 'my Adamic nature'?" Dreama asked. She was finding out things she didn't know were there. We refilled our mugs and went on.

"Well, Dreama, the Bible tells it this way. According to the first two chapters of the Bible, God created Adam because He wanted to have someone like Himself for a family. He gave Adam His own character and personality, including free will.

"Since Adam had a free will, he chose to walk and talk with God. Then God said that it is not good for man to be alone, so He gave Adam the gift of a lovely woman suitable for the perfect man, to be his mate."

"Eve," Dreama put in.

"Uhuh. The Bible doesn't say how long they had a perfect relationship with God and with each other in the Garden of Eden. One day, though, Satan came along. Adam and Eve listened to Satan. He tempted and deceived them. He persuaded them to do the only thing that God had forbidden them to do — they ate of the tree of the knowledge of good and evil. What resulted is known as the Fall of man. You know this story, don't you, Dreama?"

She nodded, but said, "Go on. I never connected it with me, though, or any kingdom of darkness."

"This is the connection, Dreama. When they disobeyed God, in that instant, Adam and Eve abandoned their kinship with God and took on the spiritually dead, rebellious nature of Satan. They looked the same, but God had said, *'for when you eat of it you will surely die'* (Genesis 2:17). And the spirits of Adam and Eve, hidden inside of them, died that day.

"When they obeyed the serpent, Adam and Eve became slaves of their new master, Satan, whose realm is the kingdom of darkness. The Bible says we are slaves of the one we obey (see Romans 6:16).

Ground Level Christianity

"This is pretty heavy, Dreama, but you don't have to take my word for it. Paul explains it this way..." I reached for my Bible and read: *"As for you, you were dead in your transgressions and sins ... when you followed the ways ... of the ruler of the kingdom of the air, the spirit who is now at work in those who are disobedient ... gratifying the cravings of our sinful nature and following its desires and thoughts ... by nature objects of wrath"* (Ephesians 2:1-3).

Dreama followed the words and the logic. "Those 'cravings of the sinful nature' and bad thoughts have ruled me and all the people I know all my life," she said. "I know that part. I want to get to the good part."

"I'm sorry, Dreama, but it takes some time to get to the good part. After the Fall, Adam fathered an imperfect, sinful race, having his fallen nature, not the nature of his heavenly Father. In spite of this, ever since, God had been seeking to bring men back to Himself, so we could be like Him.

"Dreama, is this too long a story for you right now?" She said no, so I poured more hot coffee and carried on.

Soon Dreama was ready with a fresh question. "That was such a long time ago. How do we get to today?"

"Bear with me for a minute, and then we'll get to Jesus and today. Under the Old Covenant of the Law, which was given through Moses, the sins of the people were covered by the blood sacrifice of bulls and goats. It covered the sin, but couldn't prevent it. Yet without the shedding of blood there is no forgiveness of sin, God told Moses.[3] The regulation foreshadowed what God would do to fix Adam's failure: God would send a second man (His Son, Jesus) to be a sacrifice for all sins and to provide the way for people, you and me, to have a new nature, one without innate sin.

"Only God could have been so unselfish. He sent Jesus to be the spotless Lamb, the *'Lamb of God, who takes away the sin of the world'* (John 1:29). This is what Jesus did when He allowed Himself to be crucified on the cross outside Jerusalem. He was the blood sacrifice."

"You mean, like the bulls and goats?" she asked, amazed.

Dreama Meets the Master

"Yes, Dreama. God required it, and then He supplied it, once, for all people. After Jesus' death, He was buried in a sealed tomb for three days. Then His followers found the tomb opened, and you know the Easter story. God had taken Jesus' dead body out of the tomb and given Him a resurrected body with new life — eternal life."

"I believe all this, but how can we know it, for sure?" Dreama asked.

"Well, historians who were living at that time, like Josephus, wrote about the crucifixion, and some documented the resurrection. Of course, several of the gospel writers were eyewitnesses. Paul tells about the resurrection, too."

I thumbed to the place in Paul's letters where he says: *"... of first importance: that Christ died for our sins ... that he was buried, that he was raised on the third day ... and that He appeared to Peter, and then to the Twelve. After that, he appeared to more than five hundred of the brothers at the same time, most of whom are still living ... . Then he appeared to James, then to all the apostles, and last of all he appeared to me also..."* (1 Corinthians 15:3-8).

"Paul saw Jesus on the road to Damascus, remember? We need to be sure of the resurrection of Christ, Dreama, because it's central to our faith."

"Okay."

"Once Jesus paid the price for our sins, He opened the way for us to have a new nature — not like that of fallen Adam — but like our new Father, God. Like His Son, Jesus."

"Oh, now I see why you had to tell the whole thing!"

"Yes, Jesus made a way for God to have a people for His own family — not just one or two, like Adam and Eve, not just the Jews, from Abraham — but anyone can come to Him by faith. Anyone can be delivered out of the power of darkness and be born into the Kingdom of God's dear Son — like you and I have been.

"The corrupt nature was in us, too, Dreama, as you know from looking around you. Like the Children of Israel, we need a miracle to change us too, so that we can be like Jesus."

"I know I do," Dreama sighed.

"That's what the New Birth is all about," I assured her. "Now your loyalty is to Jesus. Now you have a new hunger for the things of God. That's why you want to hear all this. It's your new heritage."

Dreama beamed. She took in a deep breath and let it out with a smile.

"I've always wanted to understand, Miz Gravely," Dreama drawled with her mountain courtesy, "but nobody ever took the time to explain so I could get the picture."

It was my turn to smile.

"One last thing is in the picture, Dreama. Jesus explained the difference between physical birth and spiritual birth to Nicodemus. He told Nicodemus that he had to be born again or he could not see the kingdom of God — ever (see John 3:1-21). This new birth happens the instant we choose Jesus to be the Lord of our life and tell Him so."

My Bible came out again and we read together: " *'The word is near you; it is in your mouth and in your heart, that is, the word of faith we are proclaiming: That if you confess with your mouth, 'Jesus is [my] Lord,' and believe in your heart that God raised him from the dead, you will be saved. For it is with your heart that you believe and are justified, and it is with your mouth that you confess and are saved. As the Scripture says, 'Anyone who trusts in him will never be put to shame.'* [Isaiah 28:16] ... *'Everyone who calls on the name of the Lord will be saved'* [Joel 2:32] (Romans 10:8-11 and 13).

"I'm showing you this, Dreama, because you need to know what the Bible says. You need to understand that you did what the Bible tells us to do. The devil may try to talk you out of it, but you have God's Word on it. You are saved."

Dreama was an eager student. She studied the words, comparing them with her actions.

"Look at me, please, Dreama," I asked when she finished. She turned from the Book. Her eyes looked straight into mine. They were full of light. A new depth and luminosity shone out of her spirit. "How do you feel?"

"Oh! I feel like I can breathe! I'm not weighted down any-

Dreama Meets the Master

more. I feel wonderful! I've always wanted to be a Christian. Now I know why!

"When I came into your house this morning, I didn't know if I could face one more day. I've got so many problems, and nobody to help me! Now I feel like God can help me — that He *will* help me — that I'm His child and He is really my Father.

"I never knew my real father, and Buck hasn't been able to be much of a father to our children, although he loves them more than anything in the world. Now I've got a Father who cares about all of us, and I don't have to carry the whole burden alone anymore! I feel wonderful!"

Our kitchen table conversation wasn't over until she unloaded all her sins on Jesus, asking His forgiveness. She was clean. Then she forgave all who had sinned against her. That day God gave her a new life: *"a crown of beauty instead of ashes, the oil of gladness instead of mourning, and a garment of praise instead of a spirit of despair. [She] will be called [an] oak of righteousness, a planting of the* LORD *for the display of his splendor"* (Isaiah 61:3).

Not long afterwards Dreama and I looked in on another conversation — the one between Jesus and Nicodemus about the consequences of not choosing Jesus. In the Gospel of John, Jesus and Nicodemus discussed this problem of not making the choice.

For God so loved the world that he gave his one and only Son, that whoever believes in him shall not perish but have eternal life. For God did not send his Son into the world to condemn the world, but to save the world through him. Whoever believes in him is not condemned, but whoever does not believe stands condemned already because he has not believed in the name of God's one and only Son. This is the verdict: Light has come into the world, but men loved darkness instead of light because their deeds were evil. Everyone who does evil hates the light, and will not come into the light for fear that his deeds will be exposed. But whoever lives by the truth comes into the light, so that it may be seen plainly that what he has done has been done through God (John 3.16-21).

"It doesn't seem fair," Dreama protested, "that someone

would go to Hell for not knowing about these Bible verses, or the ones in Romans about confessing with your mouth that Jesus is your Lord." Dreama's eyes grew big, then sad. "What about Buck," she asked. "What about Mama? What about my children? They don't know they can choose Jesus. They don't know they have to choose Jesus."

"They will after you tell them, Dreama. I believe that God works in families, and He has begun with you!"

Dreama looked hopeful — then suddenly hopeless. "Miz Gravely, I can't remember all this to tell my family. Isn't there a shorter way?"

When I laughed, she laughed, too. We laughed until our sides hurt, and she wiped her eyes with a new joy and freedom.

"Yes," I gasped when I got my breath. "Just read them 1 Corinthians 15:3-6[4] — the Gospel in a nutshell — and see that they believe in the resurrection of Jesus. The power is in the Gospel.[5] Then take them to Romans 10[6] so they can speak for themselves, confessing Jesus as their Lord, just like you did."

Dreama penciled a note with the scriptures, then looked up with a smile. "I guess God wants them 'in' even more than I do. I'll try."

Endnotes: Dreama Meets the Master

1. Philip Brooks: "O Little Town of Bethlehem"
2. **Colossians 1:13-14**—For he has rescued us from the dominion of darkness and brought us into the kingdom of the Son he loves, in whom we have redemption, the forgiveness of sins.
3. **Hebrews 9:22** states that the law requires that nearly everything be cleansed with blood, and without the shedding of blood there is no forgiveness.
4. **1 Corinthians 15:3-6**—For what I received I passed on to you as of first importance, that Christ died for our sins according to the Scriptures, that he was buried, that he was raised on the third day according to the Scriptures, and that he appeared to Peter, and then to the Twelve. After that, he appeared to more

Dreama Meets the Master

than five hundred of the brothers at the same time, most of whom are still living ...

5. **Romans 1:16**—I am not ashamed of the gospel, because it is the power of God for the salvation of everyone who believes ...
6. **Romans 10:8-13**—But what does it (the righteousness that is by faith) say? "The word is near you; it is in your mouth, and in your heart," that is, the word of faith we are proclaiming: That if you confess with your mouth, "Jesus is (my) Lord," and believe in your heart that God raised him from the dead, you will be saved. For it is with the heart you believe and are justified, and it is with your mouth that you confess and are saved. As the Scripture says, "Anyone who trusts in him will never be put to shame." For there is no difference between Jew and Gentile—the same Lord is Lord of all and richly blesses all who call on him, for, "Everyone who calls on the name of the Lord will be saved." (Joel 3:2).

Dreama on Fear and Peace

"Daytimes I run too fast for fear to catch up with me, but at night sometimes I can't get to sleep worrying, or I wake up in the night with all my children's problems right up front. When I get anxious about them the terror creeps up on me.

"I've learned not to lie there and suffer, but just to get up and read the Word until the peace comes. That peace from God is so wonderful. It's so wonderful that I'd serve God for the rest of my life for it if there were no Heaven to go to.

"You know how the Bible says that a thousand may fall at your side, and ten thousand at your right hand, but it can't touch you? Well, that's the peace that guards your heart and mind. It's worth a million dollars."

Chapter 3

Now, About the Bible...

The Bible is different from any other book in the world. It reveals who God is. It tells how He relates to us and how we relate to Him. With Bible in hand, we can actually pull up a chair and visit with our Creator and Father. We can really get to know Him.

God wants His children to know Him so He wrote Himself down in a book — the Bible, the Holy Scriptures, a living book. Christians are people of The Book.

God uses words to create continuously. Peter says that we are born of the incorruptible seed of the Word of God (see 1 Peter 1:23). As we read and meditate in the Bible, we are being transformed by the renewing of our minds, so we can prove (test and live out) the good, acceptable and perfect will of God (see Romans 12:1-2).

So the Bible is a deep book, a creative and life-giving book, but even read casually it is a thrilling book. We see God constantly connecting with individuals in the Bible stories, and He connects with us as we read and connect with Him.

Though the Bible has at least forty-four different authors, all of them were inspired by the Holy Spirit as they wrote (see 2 Timothy 3:16). The Bible has sixty-six different and distinct pieces of writing — usually referred to as "books." Some of them are short letters, while others are poetry or historical accounts. The Bible is divided into books, chapters and verses for the sake of convenience. Each verse is numbered to make it easier to find.

The Bible has two basic sections called the Old Testament and the New Testament. In general, the Old Testament is the history, laws, poetry and prophecies concerning the Jewish people, who were entrusted with the knowledge of the

Now, About the Bible ...

one true God and with the preservation of the Holy Scriptures. In the Old Testament, God revealed Himself as Creator and covenant lawgiver, as the judge of wickedness, the giver of mercy and the God who has a plan for the redemption of mankind.

In the New Testament, Jesus is the central personage — God incarnate — born into the world. In Jesus, God revealed Himself as loving Father, Redeemer (the one who took the penalty for all men's sins), Savior and Friend. Still, God's characteristics in the Old Testament are not changed, just illuminated.

In the first part of the New Testament are the four accounts of Jesus' life. Then the way the Christian church developed is told. Letters of instruction and encouragement to His followers helped the new churches then and guide us today. Finally comes the Book of Revelation, which promises the return of Jesus for the completion of history.

The Bible is not much longer than *Gone With the Wind*, but I never read it through, and I knew less about it than I did the novel. When I began to feel the need to dig into the Bible, I didn't know even these basic facts, so it didn't make much sense to me, and I was too proud to ask. Perhaps this brief resume and the brief sketch of the Bible in the appendix will help other beginners to understand the way the subjects are presented in the sixty-six books of the Protestant Bible.

Chapter 4

The Bible Is Alive!

Sometimes, in my first two-year reading of the Bible, I felt like a blind man in a dark room groping about, hoping to touch something recognizable. The only scriptures familiar to me were ones we had sung in the anthems in choir. Oh, how delighted I was to come across an old friend! Sad to say, after I touched it, I never knew where to find it again. So I went back to groping in the dark.

Why couldn't I get hold of the Bible? Even after that first reading, I didn't have an overview of what the Bible was all about. Too many bits and pieces.

One piece that made my heart thump was when Jesus spoke to the travelers on the road to Emmaus: *"And beginning with Moses and all the Prophets, he explained to them what was said in all the Scriptures concerning himself"* (Luke 24:27).

Suddenly I felt I was there! Jesus was telling me about Himself — just what I had wanted to know! *"He said to them, ... 'Everything must be fulfilled that is written about me in the Law of Moses, the Prophets and the Psalms.' Then he opened their minds so they could understand the Scriptures"* (Luke 24:44-45). I wanted Him to open my mind so I could understand, too, and I began to ask for that in my prayers.

Just in time, I found that the Word of God is *"living and active"* — the King James Version says *"powerful"* (Hebrews 4:12) — more powerful than the arthritis which threatened to cripple me twenty years ago. It happened like this:

Crippling Arthritis

Suddenly one morning I awoke, stiff and with pain in my

The Bible Is Alive

joints. "Ooooh — ouch!" I groaned when I tried to straighten out my fingers, which were clenched in a fist.

"Arthritis!" shouted my brain.

"Oh, no! I'm too young for this!" whined my vanity. *Fifty-two is much too young to be hobbled by stiff joints,* I thought.

While cooking breakfast, however, I couldn't hold onto the frying pan. It fell out of my painful grasp, and I couldn't squat to pick it up without screeching from the pain in my knees. "Jesus, help me!" I moaned.

By this time I had learned as the children's song goes, "Every promise in the Book is mine." God was teaching me to rely on the Scriptures — to let Him take over the problem while I leaned on His promise.

Soon I discovered in the book of Job a statement that electrified me. I turned it into a prayer: *"... Thou hast strengthened the weak hands. Thy words have upholden him that was falling, and thou hast strengthened the feeble knees"* (Job 4:3-4, KJV). Just what I needed for those aching joints!

In the margin of my Bible beside this verse I wrote the date of this prayer. God had thrown out the lifeline to me in the form of this promise. I didn't realize at the time that these words were spoken about Job and his good works. Instead I attributed them to God thinking that He had helped someone exactly like me. My heart swelled with gratitude and hope.

Right next to the verse, my marginal reference pointed to Isaiah 35:3-4 as a related scripture. When I looked it up, I knew it was for me. It said: *"Strengthen ye the weak hands, and confirm the feeble knees. Say to them that are of a fearful heart, Be strong, fear not: behold, your God will come ... and save you"* (KJV). I took the admonition straight to my fearful heart to be strong and fear not; my God would come and save me!

I found the clincher in Hebrews 12:11-13. It told me: *"Now no chastening for the present seemeth to be joyous, but grievous: nevertheless afterward it yieldeth the peaceable fruit of righteousness unto them which are exercised thereby. Wherefore lift up the hands which hang down, and the feeble knees; and make straight paths for your feet, lest that which is lame be turned out of the way; but let it rather be healed"* (KJV).

Hallelujah! The first scripture addressed my problem and provided a reason to pray to God about my weak hands and feeble knees. The second scripture told me I had a responsibility to be strong and fear not, but to believe God for the impossible. And the third scripture told me that in the meantime this would work in me the *"peaceable fruit of righteousness,"* as I was *"exercised"* by the chastening. ("Exercised" is the King James expression for "motivated" — like a two-by-four applied to the south end of a northbound mule!)

Furthermore, as I was *"exercised by the chastening,"* God began revealing to me things about myself that I had not noticed before: a martyr complex, pride and other emotional maladjustments. It was easy to recognize these things in others, but I had overlooked them in myself.

Praying the Scriptures

From then on, every day I prayed with faith using these scriptures, believing God would do what I couldn't do. Later on, in the Psalms I found that God has magnified His Word above His name (see Psalm 138:2) and, in Jeremiah 1:12, that He watches to make sure His Word is fulfilled. My part was to hold on tight to God's promise with unwavering faith, and He would validate His Word and bring it to pass.

One spring day, more than two years later, I realized that I could go down stairs in comfort and even squat instead of stooping. I flexed my hands rapidly without pain, and began to shout for joy. The physical symptoms which had taken fifty-two years to develop had been washed away by Jesus in less than three. And I hoped that with them had gone some of the resentment and self-pity I had come to associate with those creaking joints.

In the meantime, He had led me to take stock of those destructive emotions. I couldn't see them until He showed me. Then He gently cleansed me of these sins.

Sins? Again? Meanwhile the Lord taught me the impor-

The Bible Is Alive

tance of 1 John 1:9 which says that if we confess our sins He will forgive and cleanse us of all unrighteousness — all unrighteousness. Understandably, it would take a while to do it.

God could have healed me two years earlier, just as soon as that prayer of faith formed in my heart, but in His wisdom and love, He gave me more than just healing of the painful arthritis. During this time of suffering, He patiently taught me to believe His Word, regardless of whether the symptoms of arthritis persisted or not. The Word said that my God would come and save me, and He did.

God walked through every one of the nine hundred and eighty-two days with me until the arthritis was gone. He let me know Him in a deeper way. He showed me how to live in contentment while He takes care of both the problem and hidden sins.

Power for Any Age

There is no age discrimination in the power of God's Word, as Bessie Carr's experience showed me.

Bessie died several years ago, but many who knew her didn't know that God had given her a new body when she was well past eighty. This is her story of healing.

Bessie was a Methodist minister's daughter. Memorizing scripture was required in her home, and she still could recite it when she came to prayer group eight or ten years ago.

She had endless funny stories to tell, could recite poetry by the yard, and sang all four or five verses of most hymns from memory. She loved to cook and entertain and enjoyed life. She never complained or let her children know when she was sick. After her husband, Chick, died, she lived alone, never telling anyone that one infirmity after another was piling up on her.

Bessie began coming to the prayer group that met weekly at our home because she could see that there was life there — life beyond memorized scripture, church attendance and being good. She heard prayers spoken that were not written

Ground Level Christianity

down, but recalled scripture that she had read. She learned to sing scripture choruses. She saw answers to prayers. She even prayed aloud a time or two. But she didn't tell us about her own need for prayer.

One Wednesday Bessie came to prayer group late and sat down carefully, looking unkempt and half-put-together. Later she told us why.

She said her head felt like it would explode. Even arranging her hair jiggled the roots and added to the pain, so she took a powerful headache medication. Perms and hair color had caused huge hives to erupt all over her body, so she took powerful antihistamines. Her feet had joints so swollen that she could only wear ballet slippers, so she had a pair to match every dress. One foot was so painful that she favored it and put such strain on her hip it was almost out of joint, so she took medication for the foot and hip. Arthritis in her shoulders and elbows locked up her upper body so she could not raise her hands above shoulders. More medication. Digestive problems. More medication. She had a schedule to take her pills so she would not forget or overmedicate. She even had pills to counteract the side effects of the pills.

Bessie was so crippled that she was no longer able to go up the half flight of stairs to the bedroom in her split-level house, so she slept on the sofa. In the mornings she could not reach the overhead cabinets or lift anything heavier than the two-cup coffeepot, so she could only use what was on the counter space. Still she didn't tell her children or any of us in the prayer group.

How she got into her car and drove to prayer group that day I'll never know. I'd like to say that we prayed for her and God in his mercy healed her, but we didn't, and He didn't — at least right then. Instead she hobbled out to her car (remember, she was well into her eighties, and many people that age hobble anyway) and drove to her physical therapist appointment.

Once inside the waiting room, she had two choices: sit down and wait — which meant painfully easing down on her sore hip and then, more painfully, getting up — or just

The Bible Is Alive

stand on her sore foot to wait. She chose to stand and looked for something to read. None of the magazines appealed to her. As a last resort, she picked up a maroon covered book. It was a Gideon Bible, the first she'd ever seen. "I was afraid it was written in Gideon or something other that the King James," she said. "I don't like these new translations, you know. As far as I'm concerned, God still talks King James English."

It was indeed a King James translation, so Bessie ventured to look inside the front cover. There was a whole list of problems with scripture references beside them:

If you are lonely, see... No, she wasn't lonely
If you are depressed, see... No, she wasn't depressed
If you are in need of money, see... No, she had enough money
If you are unhappy, see... No, she was not unhappy
If you are in pain, see Hebrews 12:6-13!

There it was. Definitely, Bessie was in pain. She had no trouble finding Hebrews 12, and she read it. It spoke of *"hands which hang down," "feeble knees,"* and *"lame"* feet, and concluded: *"Let it rather be healed!"*

The Bible Is Alive!

The passage had described her problems perfectly, right down to naming her hands, knees and feet, and had said, *"Let it ... be healed!"* These words had the force of a physical impact on her spirit. Bessie was so shocked she could hardly breathe. God knew. God cared. God saw her in her trouble. And God said, *"Let it ... be healed!"*

The waiting room disappeared from Bessie's awareness as the marvel of the word of God impacting her spirit, soul and body. Time seemed to wait while Bessie was caught up into her Third Heaven.

"Oh, Mrs. Carr! How long have you been waiting out here! I'm so sorry! I can take you right now." The nurse's concerned voice interrupted Bessie's bliss.

Ground Level Christianity

She led the dazed Bessie into the whirlpool area and helped her into the tub. As the warm water swirled around her body, the healing promises from the Bible whirled in her mind, soul and spirit. There was *life* in the words. The life of God bathed her inside while the warm water relaxed her outside.

When the therapy time was over, Bessie climbed out of the tub, dressed and was opening the door when the nurse came to help her. "Why, Mrs. Carr, *how* did you get out of the tub?" she exclaimed.

Bessie shrugged, still in a daze, "I just climbed out when the time was up," she said, unaware that the nurse realized it had been impossible for her to do that on her own. At home she ate a light supper and lay down to rest. The next morning bright sunshine wakened her. She had slept through the night! Pain free! She hadn't done that in many months.

As Bessie prepared her coffee and breakfast, she waited for the pain to strike. She reached one hand toward the overhead cabinet, waiting for the constrictions of agony, but there was no pain. Her unlocked shoulders enjoyed the stretch.

She ventured up the half flight of stairs. Again, no pain. Her joints moved smoothly. Her foot and knee worked again. The hip that had been strained because she favored the foot was strong once again.

No More Pills

The first we heard of this miracle was at the next Wednesday's prayer group when Bessie told it like this: "By noon the next day, I discovered that my pills and my pill schedule were still on the counter, forgotten for almost twenty-four hours. It's been years since I've gone without medication for hives and gout and headache and arthritis. I was taking so many pills I had to check them off all day long to get them all in. Habit made me look at the list to see where to begin, and then I remembered how much God loved me. He loved me a lot with all that scourging and chastening!" she laughed. "And He loved me a lot to take away all that

The Bible Is Alive

pain! And now ... Look at me!" she exclaimed, twisting her hands and fluffing her hair.

"I chose not to take the noon dose of my medications to see how I'd get along, and I was just fine! Now, for a week I've taken *no pills*. I've washed my hair, I've slept in my bed, I've cleaned my house, I've grocery-shopped, and I've come here. All with no pain!"

Well, you should have seen the prayer group rejoice!

Bessie was still dazed that God had done this mighty deliverance by the power of His Word. That Word has life in it. It says, in Hebrews 4, that: *"the Word of God is living and active. Sharper than any double-edged sword, it penetrates even to dividing soul and spirit, joints and marrow; it judges thoughts and attitudes of the heart ... . Everything is uncovered and laid bare before the eyes of him to whom we must give account"* (Hebrews 4:12-13).

That Word literally pierced into the joints and marrow and healed tissue in Bessie Carr. God saw her plight and brought her back from almost dead. Bessie lived — vigorous, healthy, sparkling, singing her hymns and regaling us with funny stories — until, at ninety-something, she went to meet the Author of the Living Word. Just because we get old does not mean that God puts us on the shelf. God got Bessie out of her medical daze, dusted her off, shined her up and gave her back to us for five more funny years. At her funeral, her large church was filled with people who laughed through tears at the delightful memory of Bessie Carr.

God used the same scripture to heal Bessie and me (and many others, I'm sure). What took two minutes for Bessie required two years for me, but we both know it was the power and the life in God's Word that did it.

The Bible is ALIVE!

Chapter 5

Finding Guidance in the Bible

God has many ways of reaching into our lives — through our hearts and minds, through prayer, through wise counsel from godly people. Right at our fingertips is the best source: the living Word of God — the Bible. It's hard, at first, to know where to look for what we need, but God honors our baby steps of faith and helps us, even when we are first starting to seek guidance in His Word.

Our son Peyton became a believer in his early teens, and his wife Kim had known the Lord since she was a child. So when major decisions arose, they knew how to find God's will for their lives. When they fell in love, Peyton asked Kim to marry him, but she couldn't say "Yes." At least not yet.

Seated in his sports car, she lowered her head to hide the trouble in her blue eyes, so he talked to the top of her shiny blond head. "I've finished my military service. I've graduated. I've got a job and a future. We love each other. You can finish college after we're married. We've got the license, the ring and your dress. Let's get married today!"

For almost three years they had been courting, always drawing nearer to this moment. *What was the problem now?* Peyton wondered.

Kim's muffled voice spoke the only words that could stop them. "Let me get alone with God to find out what He has for us."

Kim went to a secluded place with her Bible and prayed. Almost at random, she opened to the Old Testament. *What could Ezekiel have to say to Peyton and me?* she wondered. These words almost jumped off the page at her. She knew it was God: *"Therefore, son of man, pack your belongings for exile and in the daytime, as they watch, set out and go from where you are*

Finding Guidance in the Bible

to another place" (Ezekiel 12:3). That was enough. Kim returned to Peyton with assurance of God's will, and they went to her childhood church, where her pastor married them that afternoon.

They also went to the Bible to find their first home.

Several months after their wedding, they began to look for a place of their own. They searched the real estate listings for an apartment with a suitable location and within their budget of $150 a month. Kim looked at nearly a dozen places, but nothing would do. One day they came to me with an open Bible and announced, "Look, the Lord has a house for us."

"A house? Why you haven't found a decent apartment yet, let alone a house! How do you know?"

"We found it in the Bible. In Deuteronomy. And it's in the country. Listen to this: *"When the Lord your God brings you into the land … with flourishing cities you did not build, houses filled with all kinds of good things you did not provide, wells you did not dig, and vineyards and olive groves you did not plant … be careful that you do not forget the Lord … ."* (Deuteronomy 6:10-12).

"A house with a well and a vineyard must be outside the city," Peyton said excitedly. "Do you know anybody who lives in the country? Maybe they'll know of a place for rent."

Right then I called two friends who lived in the country. Yes, they knew of four places available.

The next day Kim began running down the leads and came up with one that seemed promising. They made an appointment to see the house and prayed. They armed themselves with the scripture that provided their description.

On Thursday, filled with excitement and hope, they went to meet the owners of the house in the country, Helen and Jack. Helen showed Kim the inside of the house, while Jack and Peyton walked around the yard. The three-bedroom, two-bathroom house had just been redecorated with wall-to-wall carpets, decorator draperies and a completely furnished kitchen. In the large eat-in kitchen was a sturdy but graceful table-and-chair set, a range and a refrigerator, and in the adjoining laundry stood a washer and a dryer — all new. A small, enclosed back porch served as a sewing room.

As the men talked outside, Jack explained that he and his family had been living in the house and had just finished redecorating it for themselves when Helen's mother died. They had moved in with her father to keep house for him, leaving the fresh, clean house for rent. He pointed out the brick exterior, the storm windows, the heating plant, the utility shed with a lawn mower in it, and the garden already planted with summer vegetables and fruits.

He said, "I've already turned down two couples because they weren't exactly the ones we wanted for our neighbors. We just moved over there last week." He waved his hand toward the large frame country house on the other side of the garden. On a trellis between the houses was a Scuppernong grapevine, bordering the garden, already showing signs of spring green.

"The rent is $200 a month," Jack concluded.

Peyton said, "It's beautiful, and Kim grew up in the country, so she was very eager to see the house. I'm sure we'd like it, but my top price is $150. We're just starting out, and that's all we can afford." With nothing settled, they joined the ladies.

Kim and Helen had felt an immediate kinship when they met. Helen was duly proud of her redecorating efforts, and Kim was delighted with the charming country home with all the extras, especially the fully furnished kitchen and laundry.

Jack noticed Kim's country accent and her enthusiasm. He saw his wife beaming over the bride like a ewe with a lamb. He turned on the spigot in the kitchen sink, and said, "This drain gets clogged up sometimes, but there is an outside trap to open and fix it. Yes, and the utility bill is low because this house has its own well."

Peyton's knees almost buckled with surprise when he learned about the well. The house was filled with all good things *"which they filled not."* There were *"vineyards and olive*

Finding Guidance in the Bible

trees" already planted *"which they planted not,"* and there was a well *"which they digged not!"* He knew it was the house the Lord had for them.

The two couples chatted and found more things in common as they drifted toward the door. Once outside, while the ladies were saying good-bye, Jack said, "You and Kim seem to like the house and location, and the girls get along fine. It would be worth something to us to have good neighbors. If you want it, you can have the house for $150 a month."

They moved in within the month.

Although Kim and Peyton had learned to trust scripture to guide them, their house was a constant reminder of the provision of God for them in His Word. Because they honored God's Word, He brought them into *"the land flowing with milk and honey,"* and filled their lives with *"all good things,"* including their firstborn child.

Chapter 6

Finding Fruit on the Golf Course

What is Jesus like? What will we be like when we are like Him? Jesus is love, joy, peace, patience, kindness, goodness, faithfulness, gentleness and self-control. Paul calls these the fruit of the Spirit in Galatians 5:22.[1] The Holy Spirit, who grows this fruit, transformed a trying situation into triumph for me one day on the golf course.

Sometimes I play golf with a superb gentleman in his eighties. He is slow, and he is deliberate. He takes three or four practice swings before every shot, more before putting. Sometimes he uses his handkerchief before he hits his tee shot, and his usually accurate shots go down the fairway beyond his eyesight, so he often loses his ball.

One day as we played, while he was addressing his tee shots, I busied myself quietly manicuring my golf clubs at the water buckets by each tee. Things were going more slowly than I wanted, so I prayed for patience. I looked at his preparations, and I prayed again. After about six holes, I ran out of golf clubs to spruce up and began cleaning the grass out of the cleats on my shoes. Then I ran out of patience, too. God wasn't changing *anything*.

It's hard for me to hear God when I'm blaming Him. Somehow, though, the Holy Spirit nudged me. I looked inside myself, and all at once I found out that I was impatient with God!

Faith, Patience, and Self-Control

Suddenly it dawned on me that I would never get patience looking at the problem. My only alternative was to look to God. It takes faith to believe that God knows and

Finding Fruit on the Golf Course

cares, even about a small matter like a golf game. It takes a decision of faith to let God work things out.

When I took my eyes off the problem and looked to God, He changed everything. We found all our lost golf balls, we relished the beautiful mountain scenery and lovely air, we played an adequate game and we enjoyed the half-day together. Joy, peace, goodness, kindness and gentleness ...

The moment I came to my senses and exercised a little self-control, looking with patience toward God, my joy and peace returned, making it easy to enjoy my circumstances and the people around me. What a kind, loving way for God to teach me how the fruit of the Spirit work in ordinary life! I felt like skipping down the golf course with delight.

Jesus spoke of Himself as *"the True Vine"* in John 15:1-5.[2] He said that as we abide in the Vine, we can bear *"much fruit."* The fruit will look just like Jesus — love, joy, peace, patience, goodness, kindness, gentleness and self-control in every situation — the people of God *"thoroughly equipped for every good work"* as Paul wrote to Timothy (2 Timothy 3:17).[3]

When I first read this list in Galatians 5, it seemed fairly repetitious. Then I found that these are spiritual qualities of Jesus that He wants to reproduce in the new man by His Holy Spirit. Three of the fruit of the Spirit are inward graces, three bless the way we relate to the people around us, and three are directed toward God.

Imagine having joy, peace and self-control on the inside — our souls — and beaming those virtues out into all our circumstances! Ideally, if we could relate to our family members and friends with goodness, kindness and gentleness, we would bring Heaven into all these relationships.

What's left in the list? Love, faithfulness and patience — toward God. Why should a believer act with love, faithfulness and patience toward God? We know that the First Commandment requires it. We are commanded to love God fervently.

Once Jesus was tested by an expert in the Law, who asked: *"Teacher, which is the greatest commandment in the Law?"* (Matthew 22:36). Jesus replied, *" 'Love the Lord your God with all* your heart and with all your soul and with all your mind' This is the first and greatest commandment. And the second is like it; 'Love your neighbor as yourself.' All the Law and the Prophets hang on these two commandments" (Matthew 22:37-40).

So Jesus tells us where to start, and shows us the goal: to love God — consciously, deliberately and totally. Loving God with all our might, we'll be faithful to Him, too. It is our proper response to God.

The dictionary defines faithfulness as "loyalty and constancy."[4] "Faithful" implies "continued, steadfast adherence to a person or thing to whom one is bound by an oath, duty, obligation (a faithful wife)." "Loyal" implies "undeviating allegiance to a person, cause, institution, etc., which one feels morally bound to support or defend (a loyal friend)." "Constant" suggests "freedom from fickleness in affections or loyalties (a constant lover)."

Loving God like this is a full-time job — and impossible without the Holy Spirit working in us. If I practiced such constant love toward God, my conduct would change automatically.

Patience Toward God

But what about patience, patience toward God? I learned it in principle first, then in practice on the golf course.

In practice, it works like this: I need something; I pray about it; then I look at the circumstances, wondering when they will change. When they don't change, I become impatient — impatient with God for not answering soon enough.

In principle, however, it goes like this: I need, I pray, then I look at God and enjoy Him while He is working out the answer. Then I rejoice when the answer comes. Joy, peace and self-control are mine in the meantime. Just like Jesus taught in the Sermon on the Mount: *"But seek first the kingdom of God and His righteousness, and all these things shall be added to you"* (Matthew 6:33, NKJ). Finally, I look to Him and acknowledge that He knows my need and the right time for the answer. I relax, He works and the proper fruit begins to

Finding Fruit on the Golf Course

grow in my circumstances. The best golf lesson I ever learned — and one I am still trying to master perfectly.

Jesus had love, faithfulness and patience toward God, goodness, kindness and gentleness toward people, and was filled with joy, peace and self-control all the time. That was His nature. And take heart, God is conforming us to His image so we can bear fruit like His, too.

The turning point in my golf-course lesson came when the Teacher, the Counselor, the Holy Spirit showed me what was really going on in that trying situation. What was really going on was a spiritual battle inside my mind and spirit. Who would be in control, the Holy Spirit or my unholy nature?

Paul says they war against each other in our lives (see Romans 7:23).[5] Jesus told His disciples that the Holy Spirit would lead them into all truth, and I watched while the Holy Spirit helped me see the dynamics in that soft spring sunlit game.

There is more truth to tell about the fruit of the Spirit than I've tried to cover in this brief chapter. This is only one illustration of the supernaturally natural way that Spirit-led believers can live on their way to becoming more like Jesus.

In fact, Jesus told His disciples that they would bear fruit and do greater things[6] than He had done (see also John 14:13-14, 15:7, 16, 16:23-24 and 26). They were to wait to do these things until they were *"endued with power from on high"* (Luke 24:49).[7]

Jesus not only promises to give us His own nature, but also the same power to live the Christian life that He had — the power of the Holy Spirit. Hallelujah!

Endnotes: Finding Fruit on the Golf Course

1. **Galatians 5:22**—But the fruit of the Spirit is love, joy, peace, patience, kindness, goodness, faithfulness, gentleness and self-control.
2. **John 15:1-2 and 4-5**—I am the true vine, and my Father is the gardener. He cuts off every branch in me that bears no fruit,

Ground Level Christianity

while every branch that does bear fruit he prunes so that it will be even more fruitful. Remain in me, and I will remain in you. No branch can bear fruit by itself; it must remain in the vine. Neither can you bear fruit unless you remain in me. I am the vine; you are the branches. If a man remains in me and I in him, he will bear much fruit; apart from me you can do nothing.

3. **2 Timothy 3:16-17**—All Scripture is God-breathed and is useful for teaching, rebuking, correcting and training in righteousness, so that the man of God may be thoroughly equipped for every good work.
4. *Webster's New World Dictionary of the America Language,* Second College Edition. (New York, World Publishing Times Mirroe, 1972), p.503.
5. **Romans 7:23**—But I see another law at work in the members of my body, waging war against the law of my mind and making me a prisoner of the law of sin at work within my members.
6. **John 14:12**—I tell you the truth, anyone who has faith in Me will do what I have been doing. He will do even greater things than these, because I am going to the Father.
7. **Luke 24:49**—I am going to send you what my Father has promised; but stay in the city until you have been clothed with power from on high.

Chapter 7

"You Will Receive Power..."[1]

"What is this power of the Holy Spirit that works in people's lives?" I demanded of the little magazine I gripped in my hands. I shook it as if I could wring out the answer. The small periodical, *Voice* magazine, told about the "baptism in the Holy Spirit" — the first I had ever heard of it

A friend gave me two slim issues of *Voice* magazine in the spring of 1965. My spirit leaped when I read articles by men who told what the Holy Spirit had done in their lives. My intellect resisted, but the evidence given by doctors, lawyers, a judge, engineers and respected businessmen won out. I wanted this experience.

But what did my Bible say about all this? Searching the gospels, I learned that when Jesus went to John the Baptist to be baptized in the Jordan River, He had to insist, saying, *"Let it be so now; it is proper for us to do this to fulfill all righteousness"* (Matthew 3:15).

After John had finished baptizing Jesus in water, the Lord went up out of the river. At that moment Heaven was opened and John saw the Spirit of God descending like a dove and lighting on Jesus. A voice from Heaven said, *"This is my Son, whom I love; with him I am well pleased"* (Matthew 3:17). Then Jesus was led by the Spirit into the desert to be tempted by the devil (see Matthew 4:1).

Jesus' water baptism and His Holy Spirit baptism were two separate things — both described in this passage. Jesus didn't go out into ministry until He had been fully equipped by the Holy Spirit. Then He could face every temptation in the power of the Spirit. Pentecostals and Charismatics call this experience the baptism in the Holy Spirit. Only believers — people who are born-again — are eligible to receive it.

Ground Level Christianity

In His natural birth, Jesus was born of the Holy Spirit. The Spirit was in Him from conception, but it's not so with us. We are born of the Spirit when we declare Jesus to be our Lord and Savior. At that point we have the Holy Spirit in us replacing the Adamic (or sinful) nature.

Being born again assures us that we will go to Heaven when we die and have eternal life with Jesus, but we have battles in this life in the meantime. Since Jesus knows this, He has provided us with the same equipment that He possessed to face the devil's temptations. That's what the baptism in the Holy Spirit is all about. I wanted this baptism.

The way opened when I was invited to a Full Gospel Business Men's Fellowship International meeting in the auditorium of the local college. This was the same group that published *Voice*. The speaker was Harald Bredesen. He gave his testimony, like the men in *Voice* magazine did. Until then I had never heard a live personal testimony, nor had I heard anyone speak of being born again. It was fascinating.

Suddenly in the middle of his story, Harald stopped. His voice changed from conversational to commanding in tone. He filled the auditorium with a strange language — beautiful, but not understandable.

My heart raced. Out of my eyes welled two great teardrops and plopped into my lap. They didn't come from emotion. They came unbidden right out of my spirit.

Before I could catch my breath, Harald spoke in that same strong voice in English. It was a message from God to the people in the meeting. Two more waterspouts came out of my eyes.

Tongues and Interpretation

Tongues and interpretation! Just like the Bible describes.

Harald calmly concluded his testimony. When he invited anyone who wanted to be born again to pray with him, my hand flew up. When he invited anyone who sought the bap-

"You Will Receive Power..."

tism in the Holy Spirit to come forward for prayer, I was one of the first down front.

Harold prayed for each person individually. The ones ahead of me broke out in a prayer language they had never learned, so I fully expected to do the same. But no. He prayed, and I tried. I prayed, and he prayed in tongues. Finally two little unknown words squeezed out of my mouth. I would have drowned in disappointment if I had not been flooded with joy. Joy unspeakable and full of glory! I laughed and cried and didn't care. All I wanted to do was tell Jesus how much I loved Him. The joy went home with me, where I wrote my two little words in my Bible.

Harold warned us that Satan would tell us that nothing had really happened to us. He cautioned that the devil would steal the proof of the baptism away if he could, because with the baptism in the Holy Spirit comes the power to overcome the devil.

That joy I had received spilled out in singing — in the car, in the shower — anytime I was alone. An intense love for Jesus and what He had done for me gushed out in song. Soon I realized that I was reading the Bible with understanding — as if a teacher were standing right there to help me take it in. He was. The Holy Spirit was teaching me.

I noticed a new boldness to talk about Jesus. When I said "Jesus," the hollow ring was gone. Warmth replaced stiffness and filled in the empty silence that occurred when I spoke His name in conversation. It was two years before a fluent Spirit-language came, and during that time Satan did his best to persuade me that nothing had really happened to me — that this baptism wasn't real. It was a temptation, and I had to meet it head on, with the power of the Holy Spirit.

Satan the Thief

"Satan," I declared, "you are a thief and a robber! You can't steal this from me! Jesus said that you would come to kill, steal and destroy, but my Lord comes to bring life. This baptism is His provision for abundant life. These two words are just the beginning of what Jesus has for me. Now leave me. In Jesus' name!"

That's the way I got through.

No two struggles are alike. I share mine because I can see now that it was building my faith to rely on the Word of God rather than on my feelings.

The baptism in the Holy Spirit is necessary for us today if we are to live the way God intends. To be able to witness, pray for the sick and live righteous lives, we must be immersed in the power of our Lord. We must be baptized in Him.

Some staunch believers wonder, *If all regenerated people have the Holy Spirit, why don't they all have power like Jesus?* Jesus gave the answer. After He had risen, the Lord spoke with His disciples: *"On one occasion, while he was eating with them, he gave them this command. 'Do not leave Jerusalem, but wait for the gift my Father promised, which you have heard me speak about. For John baptized with water, but in a few days you will be baptized with the Holy Spirit ... . But you will receive power when the Holy Spirit comes on you, and you will be my witnesses in Jerusalem, and in all Judea and Samaria, and to the ends of the earth'"* (Acts 1:5 and 8).

I believe that these disciples were regenerated when Jesus appeared after His resurrection and breathed on them, saying, *"Receive the Holy Spirit"* (John 20:22). Now He was telling them that there is more: the endowment of power to live the Christian life.

The second chapter of Acts describes this endowment of power, the mighty baptism with the Holy Spirit and with fire that came on the one hundred and twenty followers as they obeyed Jesus' command to *"wait for the gift."* All the Book of Acts, in fact, and the rest of the New Testament flowed out of that Pentecostal experience.

Ask, Seek and Knock

One day my friend Alice came to my kitchen seeking this Pentecostal experience for herself. Alice had her own law practice. Although she was well born, well-educated and well grounded in the Bible, she came humbly asking for God's best. Declining my offer of refreshments, she explained her problem. She was born again and had asked for the Holy Spirit, but she didn't want to get into something strange or out-of-control.

We looked into the Bible. What did Jesus say would happen if we ask for the Spirit? We read: *"So I say to you: Ask and it will be given to you; seek and you will find; knock and the door will be opened to you. For everyone who asks receives; he who seeks finds; and to him who knocks the door will be opened. Which of you fathers, if your son asks for a fish, will give him a snake instead? Or if he asks for an egg, will give him a scorpion? If you then, though you are evil, know how to give good gifts to your children, how much more will your Father in heaven give the Holy Spirit to those who ask him!"* (Luke 11:9-13).

"Alice," I said, "you're a lawyer. You can see how Jesus compares the baptism in the Holy Spirit to a fish and the lack of it to a snake. The same with an egg and a scorpion. It is that much better. And it's good, not something to fear. If we are to receive anything from God, it is by faith and the Baptism in the Holy Spirit is no exception. There are only two preconditions: you must be born again, and you must have a desire for God's fullness."

"After I ask for it, how do I know if I have received this Holy Spirit baptism?" she asked, ever the lawyer.

How Can One Know?

"One sure sign," I explained to her, "is speaking in a Spirit-given language you never learned. Remember the one hundred and twenty believers who met in the Upper Room to receive the promise? They all burst out in unknown languages. It wasn't that way for me, Alice," I confided ruefully. "It was two years before I had much vocabulary. It took faith to hold onto my two little words until the rest of the heavenly language came."

She wanted to hear it from the Bible, so we looked at some

other scriptures together concerning the gift of tongues: *"And these signs will accompany those who believe: In My name they will ... speak in new tongues"* (Mark 16:17).

We saw that speaking in tongues was a sign that caused the Apostles to recognize that the Gentiles had been baptized in the Holy Spirit: *"The circumcised believers who had come with Peter were astonished that the gift of the Holy Spirit had been poured out even on the Gentiles. For they heard them speaking in tongues and praising God. Then Peter said, 'Can anyone keep these people from being baptized with water? They have received the Holy Spirit just as we have' "* (Acts 10:45-47).

As we looked at other instances of speaking in tongues in the New Testament, we found that this gift was a frequent sign, not a rare occurrence. Then I explained, "Another way you know you have received is by faith, Alice. Are you ready to ask in faith?"

She nodded and began to pray: "Dear Jesus, I know You are the Son of God and my Savior. You are the One who baptizes in the Holy Spirit as John the Baptist said. I love You, and I want to be all that You want me to be in Your Kingdom. Please baptize me now in Your Holy Spirit, to Your glory. Amen."

We waited.

"Do you want to speak in tongues?" Alice nodded.

"Well, say so," I urged.

"Dear Jesus," she continued, "I won't feel complete until You give me a heavenly language to praise You. I want to speak in tongues."

"Wonderful! Now let's praise Him. That's the biggest part of faith — praising before we see the answer," I encouraged her.

We spoke our love out to Jesus, first in English and then in tongues. Jesus answered Alice's prayer in the most supernaturally natural way. She spoke fluently in her Spirit-given language from the very beginning. Then we couldn't stop rejoicing!

The little magazine that started my seeking opened up a whole new life of power to Alice and me — the power to tell

"You Will Receive Power..."

others about Jesus and bring them into the fullness of the Spirit that Jesus won for all who ask, seek and knock. Along with this power come the fruit and the gifts of the Spirit that make us more like Jesus in the world.

Endnotes: "You Will Receive Power ..."

1. **Acts 1:8**—But you will receive power when the Holy Spirit comes on you; and you will be my witnesses in Jerusalem, and in all Judea and Samaria, and to the ends of the earth.

Chapter 8

"...When the Holy Spirit Comes On You"[1]

During the summer after she received the baptism of the Holy Spirit unto power, Alice and I dug into the Bible for facts, evidence and a verdict on this baptism. Along with the tongues, other gifts accompany the baptism — power gifts from the Holy Spirit. We found that this baptism is as essential today for living the Christian life as it was for the early church, nearly two thousand years ago.[2]

These indispensable gifts are listed by Paul in 1 Corinthians. They are the nine specific gifts of the Spirit — although other lists are given in other places in the New Testament. The Giver of all the gifts lives in anyone who has the baptism in the Holy Spirit, so the power gifts are there when needed, as the believer acts in faith. The gifts are supplied for the building up of the Body of Christ.

The gifts are listed in 1 Corinthians 12:8-10, and instructions for their orderly use are given in chapter 14. Sandwiched in between these discussions of power is the great chapter on love, 1 Corinthians 13, which describes the highest motive for living and for seeking and exercising these supernatural gifts of the Holy Spirit.

Knowledge Is Power

Paul starts out chapter 12 with the following: *"Now about spiritual gifts, brothers, I do not want you to be ignorant .... There are different kinds of gifts, but the same Spirit .... There are different kinds of working, but the same God works all of them in all men. Now to each one the manifestation of the Spirit is given for the common good. To one there is given through the Spirit the message of wisdom, to another the message of knowledge by means*

"...When the Holy Spirit Comes On You"

of the same Spirit, to another faith by the same Spirit, to another gifts of healing by that one Spirit, to another miraculous powers, to another prophecy, to another distinguishing between spirits, to another speaking in different kinds of tongues, and to still another the interpretation of tongues. All these are the work of one and the same Spirit, and he gives them to each one, just as he determines" (1 Corinthians 12:1 and 3-11).

First, note that these gifts are for EVERY believer, not just a few. That means you and me. The gifts are for the good of those around us, not for us (though I confess that, for me, there is hardly anything in life as wonderful to experience as one or more of those gifts working in my life). If the Holy Spirit could have His way, every believer, from time to time (and fairly frequently), would be given one or more of these supernatural gifts.

Plainly stated, the power gifts are:

- The word of knowledge
- The word of wisdom
- Faith
- Gifts of healing
- Miracles
- Prophecy
- The ability to distinguish spirits (or the gift of discerning of spirits)
- Tongues
- The interpretation of tongues.

These gifts can be categorized as vocal gifts, defensive gifts and offensive gifts. Remember that all these are given for the building up of the Body of believers — for the common good.

Possibly the most controversial, but the easiest to recognize, are the vocal gifts: tongues, interpretation of tongues and prophecy. Speaking in tongues is a gift for any believer who asks for it and appropriates it by faith — as Alice did when she was baptized with the Holy Spirit.

Ground Level Christianity

There are two scriptural uses for a heavenly language:

1. In private devotions, tongues bypass the limitations of the mind, so the believer can pray a perfect prayer to God. As Paul explained in 1 Corinthians 14, *"He who speaks in a tongue edifies himself."* (verse 4), and *"if I pray in a tongue, my spirit prays, but my mind is unfruitful"* (verse 14).
2. In an assembly of believers, it is acceptable to speak a message from God in a heavenly language if the message is interpreted in the language of the hearers, Paul taught in 14:13 and 14:5. Young believers often find that the gift of tongues is the easiest of the gifts to exercise. As the entrance ramp onto an expressway allows drivers time to build up speed, tongues gives a believer experience and faith necessary to exercise the other gifts.

Interpretation of tongues, another vocal gift, is given by the Holy Spirit to make plain to the hearers the interpretation of a message in tongues. When that happens — when there is a message in tongues matched by interpretation — it is equivalent to prophecy (14:5). And, as with prophecy, the message should be "judged" or weighed by those who listen, especially by the more mature believers.

Prophecy is the most desirable of the vocal gifts, according to Paul.[3] It is God speaking to the assembly in English or the native tongue of the people present. New Testament prophecy differs from Old Testament prophecy in several important ways:

1. In the Old Testament, the Holy Spirit rested on a few anointed men, chosen by God to be the prophet for that time in that place. They exhorted, foretold events and gave wise counsel. God often confirmed their authority to speak by giving them power to do miracles, as in the cases of Moses, Elijah, Elisha, Isaiah and others.

"...When the Holy Spirit Comes On You"

2. New Testament prophecy is a supernatural gift of the Spirit and can be given to anyone in an assembly of believers, as the Holy Spirit pleases, for the building-up of the Body. It is the only gift we are encouraged to seek (14:1). Similarly, Paul said, *"you can all prophesy in turn so that everyone may be instructed and encouraged"* (14:31).
3. It should be noted that everything can be done decently and in order and that a person exercising a spiritual gift should have self control. He should be able to stop and let someone else speak under certain circumstances.
4. It should also be noted that no gift of the Holy Spirit will bring forth something contrary to the written Word of God, for the Holy Spirit does not contradict Himself.
5. New Testament prophecy is defined as *"edification, and exhortation, and comfort"* (1 Corinthians 14:3, KJV) or *"strengthening, encouragement and comfort"* (NIV). Therefore, prophecy is not supposed to foretell the future. Rather, its main thrust and result should be encouragement. Why so? Because all believers have the Holy Spirit within them to lead them into all truth,[4] and all have prayer languages to edify themselves (see 1 Corinthians 14:4). All may prophesy according to the proportion of their faith (see Romans 12:6) and, Paul says, all should *"Be eager to prophesy, and do not forbid speaking in tongues"* (1 Corinthians 14:39). *"Two or three prophets should speak, and the others should weigh carefully what is said"* (1 Corinthians 14:29). Keeping things in that kind of order will allow older believers to balance anything that is inaccurately spoken (as might be the case with inexperienced believers).

The vocal gifts come forth in the Body of Christ always for the building up of the Body. Unlike Old Testament days,[5] there is no division between priest and people in meetings described in the New Testament, mainly because ALL believers are priests. Meetings were kept in order by the elders.

After Jesus died and was resurrected, He opened access to God to every believer with no intermediary necessary. The priesthood of all believers is a major Protestant doctrine. Believers are called *"a holy priesthood"* to offer up *"spiritual sacrifices acceptable to God"* (1 Peter 2:5) and *"a royal priesthood ... [to] show forth the praises of him who ... called you out of darkness into his marvelous light"* (1 Peter 2:9, KJV). John wrote that Jesus has made us *"kings and priests unto God ... his Father"* (Revelation 1:6, KJV).

Paul is very plain-spoken about the distribution of spiritual gifts. All may speak; all share the responsibility of affirming a prophecy if the word is from God and of disallowing the word if it is not from God. All members of the Body are equally valuable and necessary to the proper functioning of the assembly (see 1 Corinthians 12:12-27). There is only one Head of the Body, and that is Jesus. And Paul says, *"We have the mind of Christ"* (1 Corinthians 2:16).

Much more can be said about all this, and many books have been written on the subject, but in short, the vocal gifts are from God by his Holy Spirit to all Spirit-filled believers to build up the individual and the whole Body of Christ.

Miracles, Healings and Faith

The power gifts of the Spirit (miracles, healing and faith, and discernment of spirits and gifts of the word of wisdom) are like platoon football: offensive and defensive teams.

Looking at the offense gifts, we see Jesus in action. They are miracles, healing and the power gift of faith. He healed the sick, raised the dead, walked on the water, fed the five thousand, caused the barren fig tree to die from the roots and told His disciples that they could move mountains with their faith.[6]

Probably believers in the Body of Christ have performed miracles similar to all of these in the two thousand years since Jesus left this legacy — His endowment of power to

"...When the Holy Spirit Comes On You"

His followers. He started the avalanche that grows in size as it moves through time: each healing, each miracle, each work of faith showing Jesus to the world.

Bookshelves are bulging with accounts of the mighty power of God in magazines and books. I, myself, have seen many supernatural events. Here are some, which I describe not to boast but because I know absolutely that they are true:

Healings: The arthritis referred to before was one of many times when my own body has been healed. I have been healed of asthma and hay fever, chronic and acute cystitis, low metabolic rate, low hemoglobin, a severe back injury from a fall on the ice and have had rapid recovery from broken bones and internal injuries from an airplane crash.

Our daughter Louise was healed of acute lymphatic leukemia when she was a child. Although the doctors gave her no hope of recovery, she is a now married and a mother of three children and is in perfect health. My husband was healed of migraine headaches, which had plagued him for thirty years. He was instantly healed of a kidney stone by the prayer of faith.

Miracles: In a well-documented miracle, God saved my life (see *Reader's Digest*, November 1982, and *Guideposts*, August 1983). He brought me safely down in my husband's airplane, which I did not know how to fly. My husband died at the controls while we were flying a Mooney 20G at 180 m.p.h., six thousand feet up. In my ignorance I scrambled the radio, cutting myself off from all human help. This miracle is the subject of my book, *Won't Somebody Help Me!*

Faith: The power gift of faith did not move a mountain for me, but God moved three large packing boxes filled with handmade furniture from Hong Kong to my house in Rocky Mount, North Carolina with no name or address on them other than the single word "Janice." This miracle is told in the chapter called "The Power of Perseverance."

These are just a few examples that show that the Holy Spirit is active today in the same way He was active in the New Testament accounts. The power gifts of the Spirit — healing, miracles and faith — alter circumstances miraculously to show the love and power of God for His children. They are given by the Spirit *"to each, severally as He wills."* They are the offensive team in action.

Defense Against the Devil

With an offensive team like that, who needs defense? We do. We need defense against the devil, because Jesus called him *"the prince of this world"* in John 12:31. Peter said, *"Be self-controlled and alert. Your enemy the devil prowls around like a roaring lion looking for someone to devour. Resist him, standing firm in the faith"* (1 Peter 5:8-9).

We can call these defensive gifts of the Spirit. They are the gift of discerning of spirits, the word of wisdom and the word of knowledge. They help us to be alert and to resist the devil.

There is a kingdom of darkness in opposition to God's Kingdom.[7] An invisible, supernatural world surrounds us all the time, orchestrated by a fallen supernatural being named the devil, or Satan.

The devil works by suggestion, putting thoughts into our minds. He was crafty enough to deceive Eve and persuade Adam, who were not fallen human beings at the time. Since then, he has practiced on hundreds of generations of mankind. He is a master psychologist of evil. He is a deceiver. The Bible also calls him *"the accuser of the brethren"* (Revelation 12:10, KJV). In fact, the devil's weapons can be counterfeits of the gifts of the Holy Spirit.

Discerning of Spirits

So how can we tell the source of any supernatural manifestation? Where is it coming from? The Holy Spirit gift of the discerning of spirits helps the believer know. Every Spirit-filled believer has this gift to warn and protect him. Peter warns us to be alert so that we will not forget to ask the Holy Spirit the source of a supernatural happening.

A warning is also given by John: *"Dear friends, do not be-*

"...When the Holy Spirit Comes On You"

lieve every spirit, but test the spirits to see whether they are from God, because many false prophets have gone out into the world. This is how you can recognize the Spirit of God: Every spirit that acknowledges that Jesus Christ has come in the flesh is from God, but every spirit that does not acknowledge Jesus is not from God. ... You, dear children, are from God and have overcome them, because the one who is in you is greater than the one who is in the world" (1 John 4:1-4).

But what if the person does not come right out and say he is against Jesus? What if it is a mixed message — some true and some false? What if the person is a baptized member of a standard-brand church and is dabbling in the occult and doesn't know that it is against God's express command? A Spirit-filled believer can ask the Holy Spirit for understanding to learn what he is dealing with. Sometimes there is a strong "yes" in the spirit (as when a prophecy or an interpretation is true), or sometimes there is a lack of peace or a lack of affirmation in one's spirit.

Sometimes there is nothing, but try again. *"Test the spirits to see whether they are from God"* means exactly that. This is the first line of defense against the enemy.

Some may say that they will avoid the false supernatural by not allowing or participating in supernatural manifestations of any kind. That may sound fine, but churches have taken that tack for years, and it hasn't blocked the devil from messing up lives and families and marriages. Avoiding the false supernatural in this way is like driving down a highway with one eye closed. The traffic is still there, but the driver is just less aware of the dangers around him.

The Word of Wisdom

The word of wisdom can keep the church or a fellow believer from falling into a trap of Satan. As in the Council of Jerusalem (see Acts 15), believers need each other in counsel to test the wisdom of an action or decision.

Jesus said in Matthew 18:16 *"in the mouth of two or three witnesses [let] every word be established."* Many times the mem-

Ground Level Christianity

bers of the Body of Christ can get the mind of Christ on a matter in which they need guidance through the word of wisdom given to several speakers. Although it is a supernatural operation, it comes out in a very natural way. No cold chills.

Often in an assembly of believers there will be a word of wisdom given which is just what everyone needs. Other times it may for one person only.

The word of wisdom and the word of knowledge keep us out of trouble. Isaiah puts the promise of guidance very succinctly: *"Whether you turn to the right or to the left, your ears will hear a voice behind you, saying, 'This is the way; walk in it' "* (Isaiah 30:21).

Gifts of wisdom and knowledge often go together, for it often takes extraordinary wisdom to present extraordinary knowledge in a way that gets past mental or emotional barriers.

All these power gifts operate by faith. *"Without faith it is impossible to please God, because anyone who comes to him must believe that he exists and that he rewards those who earnestly seek him"* (Hebrews 11:6).

People who believe that the gifts of the Holy Spirit are for a bygone age are unlikely to exercise them. You may have heard those arguments, but you must judge the question for yourself. Paul, in his closing thought about these gifts, wrote, *"Therefore, my brothers, be eager to prophesy, and do not forbid speaking in tongues. But everything should be done in a fitting and orderly way"* (1 Corinthians 14:39-40). What is your conclusion? Are the gifts for today? Are they for you?

James wrote: *"If any of you lacks wisdom, he should ask God, who gives generously to all without finding fault, and it will be given to him. But when he asks, he must believe and not doubt, because he who doubts is like a wave of the sea, blown and tossed by the wind. That man should not think he will receive anything from the Lord; he is a double-minded man, unstable in all he does"* (James 1:5-8).

There was an instance in the life of the early church when Peter exercised several of the gifts at one time. When a be-

"...When the Holy Spirit Comes On You"

liever named Ananias and his wife, Sapphira, conspired to put on a false show of personal sacrifice, Peter used the gift of discernment to see that Satan had planted the plan in their hearts to deceive the church. With the gift of knowledge, Peter knew what the plot was, and with a gift of wisdom he confronted Sapphira in a manner that allowed her one last chance to be honest. The whole story is found in the first eleven verses of Acts 5.

Perhaps this explanation of the power gifts of the Spirit is too simple, but it shows how naturally the spiritual gifts operate in the Spirit-led life.

I know of an instance in a men's prayer breakfast where the conversation seemed naturally to move to the question of cigarette addiction. The one who raised the topic had no idea that beside him sat a man who was convicted and defeated by a long-standing smoking habit. Another man told of his deliverance from smoking. All this seemed natural, but the man with the need felt it was God encouraging him to believe for freedom. A few short prayers later, the cigarette addict left the room, "walking on air," as he later said. He went to work, got rid of all of his cigarettes and was immediately free.

What had happened? It seemed natural, but it was also supernatural. How did the exact topic of need arise? The Holy Spirit gave the knowledge of what to talk about, and the Holy Spirit gave the miracle of deliverance from addiction through the prayer of one or more of the men present. The power gifts of the Spirit are for ordinary people in ordinary need.

My son Keen says his back was healed when a fellow church member prayed for him. No special feeling attended that short prayer, only some faith — and Keen won't claim he had much of that. Nevertheless, the following years have proved that at that moment a miracle of healing took place.

These gifts, which come with the endowment of power Jesus gives, are the basic essentials needed to live the Christian life, not just window-dressing or flashy attributes of certain people. You, like Alice, may have already asked for

Ground Level Christianity

and received this infilling with the Holy Spirit. Or you may want it and need to ask someone for guidance.

The best Someone to ask is Jesus — the same Someone you ask to come into your heart, be your Lord and Savior, and to forgive your sins.

This is a gift from Jesus. He is the Baptizer,[8] but salvation comes first. If, as you read this, you need forgiveness of your sins, now is as good a time as any to stop and ask God, for Jesus' sake, to forgive you. He will, if you ask.

Ask and You Shall Receive

If you are born again and desire to ask for the Holy Spirit, then consider the following scriptures:

1. Jesus' own baptism in water and His baptism with the Holy Spirit are described (Matthew 3:13-4:1, Mark 1:9-12, Luke 3:21-22 and John 1:29-34).
2. Jesus tells His followers what to do to receive the Holy Spirit unto power (Luke 11:9-13).
3. Jesus promises the Holy Spirit (Acts 1:4-8).
4. The first outpouring of the Holy Spirit on Jewish believers is described (Acts 2).
5. The Samaritans (non-Jewish believers) and Ephesians receive the Holy Spirit by the laying on of hands (Acts 8:14-17 and 19:1-7).
6. Paul receives the Holy Spirit and is baptized (Acts 9:17-19).
7. The Gentiles receive the Holy Spirit upon hearing the Gospel (Acts 10:34-48).

Fellowship

When you are baptized in the Holy Spirit and begin using your prayer language, don't try to "go it alone." Get into fellowship with other Spirit-filled believers to build up your faith and practice the Spirit-filled life. Even before your baptism has come, keep on asking until you are satisfied. Ask,

"...When the Holy Spirit Comes On You"

seek and knock until your desire is fulfilled, as Alice and I did.

Seven times Jesus told the disciples that they would do greater works than He had done.[9] It must be true. It can be true because Jesus reproduces Himself in every born-again believer. In the two thousand years since Jesus started baptizing people to be like Him, that adds up to a lot of fruit and a lot of miracles. Each time a believer is instrumental in the salvation of another, he has fulfilled Jesus' promise.

Jesus is the Baptizer and the Enabler who gave gifts to men (see Ephesians 4:8). These power gifts are chiefly for the benefit of the Body of Christ, but they are the basic equipment for the child of God to walk safely through the minefields of life.

Endnotes: "... When the Holy Spirit Comes On You"

1. **Acts 1:8**—But you will receive power when the Holy Spirit comes on you; and you will be my witnesses in Jerusalem, and in all Judea and Samaria, and to the ends of the earth.
2. **Luke 24:49**—I am going to send you what my Father has promised; but stay in the city until you have been clothed with power from on high.
3. **1 Corinthians 14:1**—Follow the way of love and eagerly desire spiritual gifts, especially the gift of prophecy.
4. **John 16:13**—But when he, the Spirit of truth comes, he will guide you into all truth.
5. **Luke 23:45**—And the curtain of the temple was torn in two. [This signified that the separation between God — in the Holy of Holies — and man — in the outer court — was destroyed forever. Through Jesus man can have instant access to God without the priest as intermediary.]
6. **Mark 11:22-23**—"Have faith in God," Jesus answered. "I tell you the truth, if anyone says to this mountain, 'Go, throw yourself into the sea,' ... it will be done for him."
7. **Ephesians 6:12**—For our struggle is not against flesh and blood, but against the rulers, against the authorities, against the powers of this dark world, and against the spiritual forces of evil in the heavenly realms.

Ground Level Christianity

8. **Matthew 3:11**—"I [John the Baptist] baptize you with water for repentance. But after me will come one who is more powerful than I, whose sandals I am not fit to carry. He will baptize you with the Holy Spirit and with fire."
9. John 14:13-14, 15:7, 16, 16:23-24 and 26

Chapter 9

Treading Through the Minefields

No battle, no victory. No victory, no conquerors. If we are to be *"more than conquerors,"* there must be battles ahead of us — battles and minefields ready to blow up in our faces. Do we have to make our way through the minefields alone and unarmed? No, *"the weapons of our warfare are mighty through God,"*[1] who provides spiritual weapons for His soldiers. Dreama, Peyton and Louise have stories of God's provisions in victory.

Dreama stumbled into a minefield in the invisible war the minute she was born again. It happened like this. Louise, our twelve-year-old daughter, heard the kitchen ring with rejoicing after Dreama met Jesus as her Savior and Lord, and she came in to join the party.

"Lay Hands on the Sick"

Dreama reminded us that she had come to clean house, so Louise took me off to a golf game. While Dreama was working, a ferocious headache sent her searching everywhere for aspirin, Bufferin, BC — anything to dull the pain. When she found nothing, she panicked, sure that this headache, like many others before, would knock her completely out.

When Louise and I returned from golfing, Dreama tried to explain about her headache through tears of pain. Louise remembered her recent bouts with pain and sickness. She shared with Dreama that God provides that believers can lay hands on the sick in the name of Jesus and that they will recover. She said, "Look at me. I'm an example of what God will do."

We showed Dreama Mark 16 where Jesus tells His dis-

Ground Level Christianity

ciples to place their hands on the sick and pray in His name.[2] We asked if she would like for us to pray for her. Crying in pain, she consented, if this was all we had to offer.

Briefly Louise and I laid hands on Dreama in the Name of Jesus and prayed a short prayer of faith. Our part was to obey the Scriptures and use this spiritual weapon. The rest was up to God. Sometime later Dreama told it to me this way: "All I wanted was an aspirin, and all you had to offer was prayer. I didn't believe in faith healing, because I had seen some phonies. I try never to be rude, but I would have run away if I could. All I could do was stand there and say yes when you asked if you could put your hands on me."

The Pain Left

"But I want to tell you that while you were praying it felt like warm oil was pouring over me, relaxing the pain. Was I in the hands of some witches? The pain I had in my head lifted, and my stomach pain left as well. I didn't know anything to do but go back to sweeping.

"When I got home I wanted to tell everybody that I was a Christian. When Buck finally came home, he got out of a taxi, walking drunk. After dinner, when I got myself and the children ready to go to church, I found two flat tires on the car. Mabel, a neighbor, took us to church. I wouldn't have gone except you made me promise, and I knew you'd be there.

"Then, at church, when the service was almost over, I stood up to tell everybody that Jesus had come into my life. Words came out in a stream I couldn't stop. I was crying and laughing, and they were crying too. I guess they knew what a battle I'd been in. It seemed like Heaven was there.

"After church I put the children to bed and went to get the tires fixed. Buck followed me to the service station and said, 'What in the blankety-blank are you doin' leavin' those children?' "

"His words bothered me so that the headache and the stomachache came back. It scared me, so I just asked the Lord to forgive me, because I feared I'd lost my healing and my salvation. When I repented, the pain gradually left me while I was waiting for the tires to get fixed.

"The pain never came back! I've never had migraine or stomach ulcers since then. God is so good.

"Miz Gravely, when I found in Revelation the words *'they overcame him with the blood of the Lamb and the word of their testimony,'* I said right out loud to my Bible, 'Oh! That's what happened to me!' "

The Presence of Angels

The Bible says that sometimes God's holy angels fight for His people. They *"excel in strength"* to perform God's word.[3] They are *"ministering spirits"* to the heirs of salvation (Hebrews 1:14).[4] They *"encamp around those who fear [God] and ... deliver them"* (Psalm 34:7).[5] Angels have charge over the believer to keep him, protect him and bear him up *"so that you do not strike your foot against a stone"* (Psalm 91:11-12).[6] Although almost always unseen, they are, nevertheless, present. Certainly that is the only explanation for what happened to Peyton in Morningside Park, New York.

In the late sixties, Peyton was a teenager, just graduated from prep school. He went to visit his brother, Keen, who was a student at Columbia University in New York City. Keen lived near the college on West 119th Street. That part of the city is called Morningside Heights, which is adjacent to Morningside Park. The park separates the college area from Harlem.

Peyton had been to New York with a school group, but never by himself. After the train brought him into the city, he went to the subway and asked someone the way to 119th Street. By mistake he got on the subway to 119th Street, in Harlem.

When he left the underground subway and emerged onto the street, he felt a little uneasy. There he was, a clean, fresh-faced kid in a plaid shirt and cowboy boots, carrying a suitcase (his wallet, containing expense money for the trip, was in the back pocket of his laundered blue jeans), surrounded by the teeming life of Harlem. His was the only white face in sight.

He looked at the street sign: 119th, all right, but the cross street was Lennox Avenue. Oh. *East* 119th. Understandable mistake. He looked around at the people hurrying by. None of them paid any attention to him at all. Well, maybe Columbia University was near. He asked, and an affable man pointed up a tree-covered hill. "It's only about a mile — through the park. Easy walking, but nobody walks through the park anymore. No subway connection across there though. Could take a taxi."

Peyton decided that he had a little spare time before he was to meet his brother, and no spare cash for a cab, so he set out walking. Soon he came to the boundary of Morningside Park. Steps led into the green, woodsy wilderness in abrupt contrast to the concrete jungle behind. On either side were high chain-link fences, probably to keep people from falling down the embankment. Instead, now drug addicts were clutching the wires and rattling them in the convulsions of their withdrawals.

Peyton stepped up his pace to leave the frightening apparitions behind, taking the stairs two at a time, and started into the park up a winding path. Soon the city sounds of Harlem were left behind, and the leafy wasteland enveloped him. He pressed on, the suitcase slowing him down.

Dodging the Derelicts

Only a few derelicts lounged on the benches that bordered the walk. They did not look up as Peyton clipped along the path. He prayed. *"Yea, though I walk through the valley of the shadow of death, I will fear no evil, for Thou art with me ... ."*

Ragged looking people in twos and threes roamed through the park aimlessly. Some of them glanced at Peyton but their blank eyes seemed not to notice him striding along so purposefully. Only a mile? It seemed like an endless green Hell strung out along a shaggy path to nowhere. Peyton re-

Treading Through the Minefields

called David's heavenly weapons: *"Thy rod and Thy staff they comfort me."* Even so, panic threatened to close his throat as his breath came shorter and his pace picked up. The suitcase dragged him back as he struggled up the hill. Would this winding path never end? The words of the 23rd Psalm reminded him that there were two angels, named Goodness and Mercy who *"shall follow me ... ."*

Danger seemed to reach out to grab his arms from the unpruned bushes along the path. At any time, any of the derelicts wandering in the park could pull out a gun or a knife, but they didn't. Peyton walked by them unnoticed.

Suddenly sunlight shafted through a break in the leafy canopy. An opening appeared. It was the end of the park! Peyton fairly ran up the last steps to the sidewalk on Morningside Drive, heedless of the weight of his suitcase or the long trek through the park. *"And I will dwell in the house of the Lord FOREVER!"*

Half a block later he was safely inside the lobby of his brother's apartment house. He sat down to wait and to try to figure out what had happened — or, more to the point, what had not happened.

What Did Happen?

What did happen? Why had everyone ignored him? He reached back to feel for his wallet. It was still there. It contained enough cash for a lot of fixes. Why was it still there? Why was he still here?

He thanked God for safe conduct through the minefield, and suddenly he remembered a story from the Bible in which Elisha the prophet and Gahazi were surrounded by the troops of the king of Aram: *"When the servant of the man of God got up and went out early the next morning, an army with horses and chariots had surrounded the city. 'Oh, my lord, what shall we do?' the servant asked. 'Don't be afraid,' the prophet answered. 'Those who are with us are more than those who are with them.' And Elisha prayed, 'O LORD, open his eyes so he may see.' Then the LORD opened the servant's eyes, and he looked and saw the hills full of horses and chariots of fire all around Elisha"* (2 Kings 6:15-17).

While the parallel is not exact, it reminded Peyton that if the Lord were to have opened his eyes, he might have seen those protecting angels around him, because something or someone must have protected him while he was surrounded and outnumbered by dangerous vagrants.

Everyone had ignored him except the man who had answered his question on the street. It seemed, too, that the Lord had closed the eyes of all the others — the people on the streets of Harlem and even the outcasts in the park — so they could not see him. Had God covered him with a supernatural cloaking device to protect him?

When Keen joined him, Peyton told the story. Keen exclaimed, "Peyton, are you crazy? Nobody ever goes into that park and comes out alive! The addicts have taken over, and they rob and kill anyone coming into their territory. Even policemen don't venture in except in twos, and they're armed. Maybe the Lord did protect you this time, but don't ever do that again!"

Our Bodyguards

Life is indeed full of pitfalls, even minefields for some. *"What shall we then say to these things? If God be for us, who can be against us?"* (Romans 8:31, KJV). We are *"more than conquerors"* in this invisible war when we know our rights and privileges as soldiers in God's army. He arms us with the mighty name of Jesus, the power of the blood of Jesus, our testimony (see Revelation 12:11), prayer, His protecting angels and all the gifts and fruit of the Spirit

So as we tread through the minefields of life, we can say with the psalmist: *"Assign me Godliness and Integrity as my bodyguards, for I expect you to protect me"* (Psalm 25:21, TLB).

Endnotes: Treading Through the Minefields

1. **2 Corinthians 10:3-5**—For though we live in the world, we do not wage war as the world does. The weapons we fight with are

Treading Through the Minefields

not the weapons of the world. On the contrary, they have divine power to demolish strongholds. We demolish arguments and every pretension that sets itself up against the knowledge of God, and we take captive every thought to make it obedient to Christ.

2. **Mark 16:15-20**—He [Jesus] said to them [the disciples], "Go into all the world and preach the good news to all creation. Whoever believes and is baptized will be saved, but whoever does not believe will be condemned. And these signs will accompany those who believe: In my name they will drive out demons; they will speak in new tongues; they will pick up snakes with their hands; and when they drink deadly poison, it will not hurt them at all; they will place their hands on sick people, and they will get well."

   After the Lord Jesus had spoken to them, he was taken up into heaven and He sat at the right hand of God. Then the disciples went out and preached everywhere, and the Lord worked with them and confirmed his word by the signs that accompanied it.

3. **Psalm 103:20**—Bless the LORD, ye his angels, that excel in strength, that do his commandments, harkening unto the voice of his word. (KJV)

4. **Hebrews 1:14**—Are not all angels ministering spirits sent to serve those who will inherit salvation?

5. **Psalm 34:7**—The angel of the LORD encamps around those who fear him, and he delivers them.

6. **Psalm 91:11-12**—For he will command his angels concerning you to guard you in all your ways; they will lift you up in their hands, so that you will not strike your foot against a stone.

Chapter 10

"But Deliver Us From Evil"[1]

Our nine-year old daughter Louise was almost dead from leukemia and toxic medication. Her father carried her in his arms across the parking lot to Duke Hospital for her second visit. Away from the security of the car, she cringed with fear as she neared the dreaded place. Four days before Christmas her doctor sent her to Duke for emergency treatment for acute lymphatic leukemia, a quick killer. Christmas Day and the week following she spent in our local hospital. Now seeing the Duke hospital buildings again, instant replay brought back to her mind the horror of the bone marrow test, the shots and intravenous chemotherapy drip and the gagging reaction to the steroids.

She whimpered as we entered the hematology laboratory for the blood sample to be drawn. There, in the small lab, her limp body propped against my chest, she swayed on a high stool while she waited for the two nurses to finish her off with the needle.

I couldn't stand it. I had to do something. Anything. *Call on Jesus!* I thought.

I gulped a breath of disinfected air and blurted, "Do you two ladies know the Lord's Prayer?"[2]

One nurse sorted blood samples as the other readied the big needle. The centrifuges whirled, and the sorters bobbed up and down while we waited for the answer. Finally the two nurses said yes and looked to see what could follow such a question in the laboratory.

"Will you say it with us, now?" I pressed on. Surprise and hesitation delayed their answer, but they agreed, if only out of curiosity.

We began the familiar *"Our Father..."* in unison, but when

"But Deliver Us From Evil"

we got to *"deliver us from evil,"* I stopped the recitation to ask Louise, "Is this fear an evil thing to you?" By now she was weeping, and what little strength she had was oozing out her eyes, but she nodded through her tears.

"Would you like to ask Jesus to deliver you from this evil? He is your strong Deliverer, you know." She nodded.

"Well, all you have to do is ask," I prompted.

So she asked in childlike faith, "Dear Jesus, please deliver me from this awful fear."

The whole laboratory — nurses, bobbing test tubes, whirring centrifuges, Louise and I — triumphantly finished together: *"For Thine is the kingdom, and the power and the glory forever. Amen."* We were almost jubilant.

Then we watched with fascination at the change that came over Louise. We could almost see the fear draining out of her. Strength flowed into her bones as the spirit of fear ebbed away. She straightened visibly. The nurses saw it, too, and we all praised the Lord just like in an old-fashioned camp meeting. They understood. We had church right there in the middle of the test tubes.

The Power of Fear

I don't know when Louise was delivered from the leukemia. It might have been that first prayer out on the sidewalk before we ever went to Duke for treatment.

Immediately after the initial diagnosis by Louise's pediatrician, I called my friend Margaret, a faithful prayer warrior, and she came at once. While Edmund had Louise in the car with the motor running (speedy treatment was crucial to her survival), Margaret and I stood on the sidewalk beside the house and prayed for her healing.[3] After we left, she marshaled "the forces" (our faithful friends) to pray. Many people prayed for Louise every day for more than three-and-a-half years.

Nearly ten days after the liberation from fear in the laboratory, Louise was anointed with oil in the name of the Lord

Ground Level Christianity

by an Episcopal rector according to James 5:14,[4] and soon after that we had an eye-popping experience.

One day she had a recurrence of a stomachache that had bothered her in the past. As weak as she was, any setback invited fear into our hearts. We had to fight this thing! Fear is the opposite of faith in God; fear is faith in the devil and what he might do to hurt you. James says, *"Resist the devil, and he will flee from you. Come near to God and he will come near to you "* (James 4:7-8). We had to resist the devil!

I whisked Louise upstairs to my bedroom to make her comfortable in my bed where I could pray for her. While I was praying some of the reassuring and powerful healing scriptures in the Word of God, a word of knowledge came to me. I discerned that the stomachaches could be brought on by self-pity operating in Louise.

The Power of Self-Pity

I waited until Louise seemed more comfortable, then I asked her, "Louise, does it make you feel a little sorry for yourself sometimes that you are sick like this?" She nodded. "Is it a little like you feel God isn't paying attention to you?"

She cocked her head as she thought it over. "Well yes, I guess so," she allowed.

"That's like doubting God, isn't it?" I probed. She followed the line of thinking, and agreed. "Doubt and faith can't both be in your thoughts at the same time, can they?"

"No."

"Well, Honey, the Bible says *'whatever is not of faith is sin,'* so I guess it's a sin to feel sorry for yourself instead of trusting that God is looking after you. Does that make sense to you?" She chewed on that thought a while, then acknowledged the problem.

"Well, we know what to do about sin, don't we? The Bible says, *'If we confess our sin, God is faithful and just to forgive our sin and to cleanse us of all unrighteousness.'* Do you want to do that and get rid of that self-pity?"

"But Deliver Us From Evil"

She certainly did want to get rid of it! In her childlike, direct way, she named the ugly thing, confessed it as sin and repented of it. In faith she asked forgiveness, and by faith received cleansing of all that unrighteousness.

All her discomfort ebbed away, and Louise yawned and settled into the pillow.

How faithful God is! I thought. *How sweet and relaxed she looks yawning like that!*

Turned Inside Out

But Louise continued to yawn without dropping off to sleep. She snuggled into the covers trying to find a sleepy spot. She yawned and yawned and YAWNED, until I thought her jaws would crack. She yawned until it looked like she would turn inside-out, all the way down to her toes. It was alarming, yet neither she nor I could do anything to stop it.

I bowed my head and prayed so she could not see my astonishment. I knew God was in it all, but I had never seen anything like this before. Louise was absolutely wrung out with yawning. At length it subsided, and she drifted into an untroubled sleep, as I watched in awe and amazement.

She never had the stomachaches again, and she was released from treatment for leukemia before five years had passed. God healed her of self-pity and leukemia in the bargain. He truly delivered her from evil. In this experience, God gently took care of several serious problems in a very supernaturally natural way. Once we identified the ground[5,6] (self-pity) which Satan had occupied for most of her young life, and confessed the sin of it, once she repented and received forgiveness, taking away that ground, then he no longer had any legal right to remain there. He had to go.

Possibly Louise was healed of leukemia at the time she was delivered from self-pity or was anointed with oil. Because her body was ravaged by the toxic medication, we don't know specifically when the healing took place. But God was faithful to heal her, and later He arranged circumstances that allowed us to stop the medication altogether.

Ground Level Christianity
Dealing With Sin

Sometimes the link between sin and sickness is clear. Some sins lead directly to worse sins, but some thought patterns or attitudes of heart can lead just as directly to physical weakness and the vulnerability to disease. In Louise's case, sin was uncovered as the sickness was being treated.

But not all sickness is the result of sin. Job had not sinned when he suddenly found himself covered from head to toe with boils. He was under satanic attack.

Jesus was asked about a man who was born blind: *"Who sinned, this man or his parents, that he was born blind?"* (John 9:2). Jesus replied that no one's sin had caused the condition.

To another man whom He healed from paralysis, Jesus said, *"See, you are well again. Stop sinning or something worse may happen to you"* (John 5:14).

Life is much more about having faith than not having sin. No man is without sin, but no one can have a right relationship with God or enjoy a healthy condition of heart and mind without true faith in Christ.

If we confront a stubborn illness, it may be that our attention needs to be drawn to some unconfessed sin or wrong attitude of heart. Some things will definitely hurt us because they are sins of the heart — hatred, anger, self-pity, envy, jealousy, greed, resentment and fear. They open the door, either for disease or Satan (or both) to work against us. Even when we are not sick, these sins warp our personalities and our thinking.

We should not rule out the possibility that a stubborn illness is related to sin. We can ask God to show the sin. Then, after dealing with any sin that is discovered, we need to carry on in a trusting relationship with God.

Healing may not come instantly. It may be a process. Sometimes it is dramatic, sometimes surprising. But even if it does not come, we know that God is good, that He loves us, that He will use all circumstances to conform us to the image of Jesus and *"deliver us from evil."*

"But Deliver Us From Evil"
Endnotes: "But Deliver Us From Evil"

1. **Matthew 6:13**—And lead us not into temptation, but deliver us from evil: For thine is the kingdom, and the power, and the glory, for ever. Amen. (KJV)
2. The Lord's Prayer is found in **Matthew 6** and **Luke 11**. The most familiar version of it is: *"Our Father, which art in heaven, hallowed be thy name. Thy kingdom come. Thy will be done in earth as it is in heaven. Give us this day our daily bread. And forgive us our debts, as we forgive our debtors. And lead us not into temptation, but deliver us from evil. For thine is the kingdom, and the power, and the glory, for ever. Amen."*
3. **Matthew 18:19**—If two of you on earth agree about anything you ask for, it will be done for you by my Father in heaven.
4. **James 5:14-16**—Is any one of you sick? He should call the elders of the church to pray over him and anoint him with oil in the name of the Lord. And the prayer offered in faith will make the sick person well; the Lord will raise him up. If he has sinned, he will be forgiven. Therefore confess your sins to each other and pray for each other so that you may be healed. The prayer of a righteous man is powerful and effective.
5. When Pilate said of Jesus, *"I find no fault in this man"* (Luke 23:4), he was saying that here was no cause, basis, or ground for him to harm Christ. If Satan cannot find a fault in us, he cannot harm us. If he can find such fault, he has cause, basis or ground to harass us. Since we are all imperfect people, and since it pleases God to conform us *"to the likeness of his Son"* Jesus (Romans 8:29, see also Philippians 3:10), Satan is just a tool to identify the ground and harass us until we root out the sin base (ground) that he has been using against us. Louise was just a little girl who had already been born again into the Kingdom of God by faith in Jesus, but Satan found grounds to harass her. What the devil meant for harm, however, God meant for good (see Genesis 50:20). In this way, God deprived Satan of that ground of self-pity, freed her and removed the block to her healing. God then healed her.
6. **Job 5:6**—For hardship does not spring from the soil, nor does trouble sprout from the ground.

Chapter 11

"Sad Hearts, Weep No More"

His Name is Jesus, Jesus!
Sad hearts, weep no more!
He has healed the brokenhearted,
Opened wide the prison door,
He is able to deliver, evermore!

Our daughter Jane and I sang this song all day to encourage our sad hearts while we were packing up her things for moving home. She had lived six years in Williamsburg, Virginia, a story-book town where anybody would love to live — but not Jane, at least not now. Her whole world had unraveled like knitting that has slipped from its needle.

Just twelve days before, she had challenged God, thumping the Bible in her hand: "If You are really who You say You are in this Book, You're going to have to DO something or I'll die!"

Less than two weeks later, her father had said, "Jane, your mother and I would like for you to pack up, bring your dog, and move home with us." She knew it was God's answer.

Six Threats to Her Life

During those six years Satan tried to kill Jane six times. First, a Japanese hornet stung her as she came down the outside stairway at her first apartment. The poison in the stinger was like a sledge hammer blow to her nervous system, and she was barely able to crawl to her neighbor's porch before she lost consciousness. Prompted by a slight noise outside, the neighbor came to the door to find Jane almost unconscious on the steps. Only the quick response of paramedics

"Sad Hearts, Weep No More"

saved her life. It was summer time, and Jane came to the mountains to recuperate.

The following summer, an employee Jane had hired to work with her turned out to be a psychopath. He robbed her office and her home of all her personal papers and left notes both places, threatening to kill her. Jane again escaped to the mountains until the man was apprehended and put under psychiatric care.

Two serious attacks on her health undermined her sense of well-being. Her work suffered and her eyesight went from a perfect 20/20 to a myopic 20/400, and her job suffered even more.

Just before her challenge to God to do something in her life, Jane drove into a ditch when her steering wheel jerked to the right. The car's axle broke, and she realized she could no longer trust herself to drive. Now she was riding with friends to and from work. No wonder she prayed, "Get me out of this, or I will die."

Lacking Fellowship

Jane was not young in the Lord. She had given her life to God at a lay-witness mission when she was thirteen. Immediately she went out as a Youth Witness, and was baptized in the Holy Spirit at a mission soon afterward. Now, at twenty-six, she had been moving in the power of the Spirit half her life. She had seen Louise's illness and healing and knew the snares of the devil and the power of God. She walked with God in prayer and faith as a way of life.

One thing was lacking in Jane's life. Of that I am sure. She had no fellowship with other Spirit-filled believers. I am convinced that this is one of the four basic ingredients for healthy Christian growth.

Jane prayed, she worshipped regularly in a denominational church, she was faithful in Bible study, thus fulfilling the other three essentials. But there was no encouragement for her life in the Spirit — no prayers for her safety through the minefields of life, no words of knowledge or wisdom to warn her, no early revelation from God to guide her path. These are the helps that members of the Body of Christ supply to one another when they meet together in fellowship.

Fellowship is God's provision for the protection and nurture of His people. Without it, Jane's spiritual resources, built up over many years, ran low, because they were not being replenished through body ministry. As a consequence, I believe, she became fair game for the devil, like a little lamb caught in the brambles, outside the protection of the flock.

On her knees now, she called out to Jesus, her Good Shepherd. He heard. He tenderly gathered her up in His arms and settled her in a place of nurture and love, moving her back to her childhood home.

As we packed up her things, we sang:

His name is Jesus, Jesus,
Sad hearts, weep no more,
He has healed the brokenhearted,
Opened wide the prison door,
He is able to deliver evermore.

My husband flew home in the plane that brought us to Williamsburg, and I drove Jane's car, because she was unable to drive.

Available Spiritual Resources

Once in Rocky Mount, at first Jane couldn't do much of anything. She was almost over the edge into the abyss of depression, crippling, debilitating melancholia. She was spiritually bankrupt.

Unlike some places, Rocky Mount has many spiritual resources, and we called on all of them. The first place of ministry for our daughter was our home. We try to make our family and home life a mini-expression of the Body of Christ. Jesus is the Head, and we all are submitted to Him and mutually submitted to one another in love — at least, that is the ideal toward which we all aim.

"Sad Hearts, Weep No More"

We pray for each other so that we *"may be healed"* (James 5:16).[1] We do not neglect to assemble with other believers (see Hebrews 10:25)[2] and we *"run with patience the race that is set before us, looking unto Jesus the author and finisher of our faith"* (Hebrews 12:1-2, KJV).[3]

We take up all our spiritual weapons, the Word of God, the Blood of Jesus, the resurrection power of God, prayer and fasting and faith and do battle with Satan, because *"the one who is in you is greater than the one who is in the world"* (1 John 4:4).[4] In the meantime, *"we are more than conquerors through him who loved us"* (Romans 8:37).[5]

Although Jane was physically weak, she and I went to church Wednesdays and twice on Sundays, attended Bible study twice a week and prayer group on Wednesdays, as well. At first, it was like dragging a beanbag out the door to get Jane on her feet to go. At home, however, she discovered the Old Testament. In a modern version, the stories made sense to her for the first time, and she read voraciously. How excited she was to discover that *"the eyes of the LORD range throughout the earth to strengthen those whose hearts are fully committed to him"* (2 Chronicles 16:9). She had always read and studied the New Testament and was well versed in the Scriptures. But now she was getting acquainted with the God of the Old Testament, the Father, and she was being *"transformed by the renewing of [her] mind"* (Romans 12:2).[6]

Practical Actions

Practical actions accompanied the spiritual ones. We had regular, wholesome meals with loving and low-key table-talk, regular bedtimes, rest after lunch, and opportunities for pleasant conversation and sharing. Lots of goodness, kindness and gentleness toward Jane was undergirded by love, faith and patience toward God. Peace, self-control and even joy began to appear in Jane, and in the rest of us, as *"[we struggled] not against flesh and blood, but against the rulers, against the authorities, against the powers of this dark world and against the spiritual forces of evil in the heavenly realms"*

(Ephesians 6:12). We rolled out the whole arsenal of spiritual weapons to rally around Jane in love.

Professional help from a Christian psychiatrist gave Jane new coping techniques that she practiced on us, and when they worked, she shared them with us. One approach she used was assertive behavior, as opposed to aggressive or passive behavior.

Another practical action was the honest identification of sin and confession of it as sin. This leads to forgiveness of the sin and freedom from its bondage. Jane systematically deprived Satan of his base of operation against her, and he had to leave. Instead of being treated in the hospital or with drugs, as the psychiatrist first recommended, Jane trudged out of the Valley of the Shadow with the help of Jesus and her own fixed determination. As Paul declared, *"If God is for us, who can be against us?"* (Romans 8:31).

Two weeks after Jane came home, my husband told her she needed to get a job — any job — so she got a job as a substitute math teacher at a local high school. Bible studies were her spiritual food, so she prayed that God would order her work to include them. Somehow she was called for work only on the days with no scheduled Bible studies. Each day was an ordeal, trying to cope with her fragile emotions and all the people she encountered in the schools.

After about three months, Jane began taking courses in computer science at the local technical college. Before long she was teaching classes in computer, taxes and basic math and English at the Community College.

Without hospitalization or medication, Jane got well. God DID something in answer to her challenge! It was *"exceeding abundantly above all that we [could] ask or think"* (Ephesians 3:20, KJV). Best of all, in the meantime, she developed a new relationship with the Father and the Son.

> *His name is Jesus, Jesus*
> *Sad hearts, weep no more;*
> *He has healed the brokenhearted,*
> *Opened wide the prison door,*
> *He is able to deliver evermore!*

"Sad Hearts, Weep No More"
Endnotes: "Sad Hearts, Weep No More"

1. **James 5:13-16**—Is any one of you in trouble? He should pray. Is anyone happy? Let him sing songs of praise. Is any one of you sick? He should call the elders of the church to pray over him and anoint him with oil in the name of the Lord. And the prayer offered in faith will make the sick person well; the Lord will raise him up. If he has sinned, he will be forgiven. Therefore confess your sins to each other and pray for each other so that you may be healed. The prayer of a righteous man is powerful and effective.
2. **Hebrews 10:25**—Let us not give up meeting together, as some are in the habit of doing, but let us encourage one another—and all the more as you see the Day approaching.
3. **Hebrews 12:1-2**—Therefore, since we are surrounded by such a great cloud of witnesses, let us throw off everything that hinders and the sin that so easily entangles, and let us run with perseverance the race marked out for us. Let us fix our eyes on Jesus, the author and perfecter of our faith, who for the joy set before him endured the cross, scorning its shame, and sat down at the right hand of the throne of God.
4. **1 John 4:4**—You, dear children, are from God and have overcome them, because the one who is in you is greater that the one who is in the world,
5. **Romans 8:37**—No, in all these things we are more than conquerors through him who loved us.
6. **Romans 12:2**—Do not conform any longer to the pattern of this world, but be transformed by the renewing of your mind. Then you will be able to test and approve what God's will is—his good, pleasing and perfect will.

Some fundamental truths to be gained:

Jane's story illustrates some fundamental truths in the Christian life:
1. The first is that everything that can happen to us has been covered in the atoning work of Jesus in His death and resurrection.

Ground Level Christianity

2. Things that happen to a Christian are not random chance or bad luck, but are being *"worked together for good"* (Romans 8:28) if we love the Lord. They are for the purpose of conforming us to the image of Jesus (see verse 29).
3. Believers thrive in fellowship and wither outside the Body of Christ. In the Christian life there must be no Lone Ranger. Each one is an indispensable member of the Body of Christ and cannot function alone for very long. Meeting together is essential for growth and accountability. In addition to fellowship, each believer needs to have regular Bible study, prayer and worship. These four aspects strengthen the Christian walk throughout life.
4. **Isaiah 59:19**—When the enemy comes in like a flood, the Spirit of the Lord will life up a standard against him (NKJ).
5. When we call out to God, help will come. Be looking for it.
6. Jane's depression was an illness from Satan, a demonic attack, which, if left alone, could have killed her. Satan came to kill, to steal and to destroy, but Jesus came to bring life, and that, abundantly (see John 10:10).
7. Deliverance from such attacks is covered in the atonement.
8. Walking through this experience with Jane taught us how far-reaching the atonement of Jesus is for us. It is presumptuous to try to deal briefly with the meaning of the suffering, crucifixion, death and resurrection of Jesus. But with that apology, I'll try. Isaiah states in a few words the scope of the atonement:

> *He was despised and rejected by men,*
> *a man of sorrows, and familiar with suffering.*
> *Like one from whom men hide their faces*
> *he was despised, and we esteemed him not.*
> *Surely he took up our infirmities and carried our sorrows,*
> *yet we considered him stricken by God,*
> *smitten by him, and afflicted.*
> *But he was pierced for our transgressions,*
> *he was crushed for our iniquities;*
> *the punishment that brought us peace was upon him,*
> *and by his wounds we are healed.*
> *We all, like sheep, have gone astray,*

"Sad Hearts, Weep No More"

each of us has turned to his own way;
and the Lord *has laid on him the iniquity of us all.*
                                                           Isaiah 53:3-6

Verse 6 means (at the very least) that Jesus atoned for the Fall and for our fallen nature. When we declare Jesus Lord of our lives, and He becomes our Savior, the sin price is paid, and we are saved by grace — by faith alone and not by any works we have done (see Ephesians 2:8). After that, we can willfully do as Jane did: go our own way. For this, too, there has been payment made, when we confess our sins, according to 1 John 1:9.

Verse 4 gets specific. *"Infirmities,"* according to Webster, include "physical weaknesses or defects, frailties or ailments," even "moral weaknesses." Jesus took them up and carried them, along with our sorrows. We don't have to. Many times we mistakenly carry them by choice, even though Jesus is able to carry them, and we are not.

Verse 5 might sound poetically repetitious for emphasis. It isn't. The Bible distinguishes between iniquity and transgression in the same way as "the thought is father of the action." David said, *"If I regard iniquity in my heart, the Lord will not hear me"* (Psalm 66:18, KJV), a theme echoed in Job 27:8-9, Proverbs 28:9 and in other passages as well.
Isaiah puts it this way:

Their feet run to evil,
And they make haste to shed innocent blood;
Their thoughts are thoughts of iniquity;
Wasting and destruction are in their paths.
                                                           Isaiah 59:7, NKJ

Jesus was crushed for our iniquities. It took all of that crushing to pay for the iniquities, but we have to crush them out, too. Paul refers to it as putting *"the old man"* under (see 1 Corinthians 9:27, KJV). By conscious effort and desire, we walk in the newness of life of the new man with the Jesus nature (see Ephesians 4:22-24).

In addition, Jesus was pierced for our transgressions, our sinful acts stemming from the evil that is in us, the iniquity. These acts, when confessed, are forgiven and forgotten by God because Jesus was pierced in His side and shed His blood in payment for them.

Last, the punishment that brought us peace was upon Him: peace of mind, mental health. Healing of mental illness and depression was obtained for us by that terrible punishment. People with mental illnesses and depression suffer terribly, but it need not be so. Jesus suffered terribly so they would not have to. Unfortunately, the passive attitude that often accompanies depression makes it very hard for the victim to be transformed by renewing his mind. He is too depressed to make the effort, and Satan keeps piling on the depression and/or other mental illness. But sufferers can take heart because *"BY HIS STRIPES WE ARE HEALED."* The Bible says it, I believe it, and that settles it.

Chapter 12

"They Will Drive Out Demons" [1]

Do evil spirits really exist in this enlightened age? Do they afflict people as they did in Bible days? Do they seek to inflict harm even to believers? Absolutely! Katie was a child who needed deliverance from evil spirits, and God made a way for that to happen.

One Sunday, after coming into the morning worship service in our large downtown church, I sat next to my friend Barbara and was surprised to find her crying — right there in church. "What's the matter, Barbara? Did something happen in Sunday school?" I asked.

She lifted her head and looked searchingly at me. Normally fair, her face was puffy, and she had red eyes and nose. "It's Katie," she blurted out. "She has tormented all of us unbearably lately. She fights with Heather and tortures the twins when we're not looking. She defies Bob and me. It was all we could do to get to Sunday school today.

"Janice," she asked hesitantly, "do you think a child can be demon-possessed?" When I nodded that I did, she continued her story.

"Katie isn't just naughty, she is *evil*. EVIL! Bob and I pray. We are kind and firm and try to be evenhanded with the children, but we can't stay ahead of Katie. She lies and does things no ordinary child could come up with. It's horrible to have her in the home! There is no peace anymore. I don't know what to do, and I can't stop crying. Can you help?"

She broke off the question as her six-foot, six-inch husband joined us in the pew with Katie and Heather. "The twins are in the nursery and seem to be okay," he said, as we scooted over to make room on the long pew, and the chimes proclaimed the beginning of the worship service.

Ground Level Christianity

During the opening hymn I recalled what Barbara had told me of her past. After the breakup of her first marriage she was left with two-year-old Heather and was expecting a second child. Alone in Atlanta, Georgia, she was searching for meaning in her life. A helpful co-worker invited her to a meeting where she could ask direction from the kind lady who held a weekly seance. She seemed to have some answers, so Barbara continued to go to the friendly circle and began to read books about spiritualism.

Suddenly something happened to change Barbara's mind. She told me that she was riding the bus to the spiritualist meeting one day with her "lap full of babies" when a voice spoke to her out loud: "If you go to this meeting, Barbara, you will never be free again."

She jerked her head around to see who had spoken. It was no one on the bus. She told me that the impact on her was so great that she sat immobile when the bus stopped at her meeting place. She doesn't even remember how she got home because the bus took her clear to the end of the line. She never went to a seance after that. Instead she turned to her Episcopal church for answers and emotional support.

Barbara's second daughter, Katie, was born to a lonely, rejected, angry and frightened twenty-two-year-old single mother. She was too proud to reach out to her parents, but they helped her financially until she could get on her feet and get a job.

As it happened, in her church there was a mother-figure who led Barbara to the Lord, bringing the security into her life of the One who would never leave her or forsake her (see Hebrews 13:5).

She met Bob at her job and, after a brief courtship, they were married. Twins were born before their first anniversary. Bob summarized his life, saying, "In eleven months I went from being a happy, carefree bachelor to the head of a family of six. That makes you grow up fast."

Soon Bob's job brought them to Rocky Mount. Bob's traditional roots prevailed in their choice to come to our church, where I met them. Barbara and I worked together in Girl Scouts.

"They Will Drive Out Demons"

On a visit to Atlanta, Barbara heard about the baptism in the Holy Spirit and joyfully received the gift from Jesus, the Baptizer. When she returned to share with Bob, he couldn't understand any of it. Barbara, however, turned up in our prayer group with twin babies in her arms. From that time on she matured steadily in her Christian walk as she and Bob built a stable family life together. The biggest snag was Katie.

Could Katie have a demon? Seated that morning in the fifth pew, I questioned God during the singing of the first hymn. It certainly seemed possible, in light of the conditions surrounding her while Barbara was pregnant. Hatred, anger, rebellion, rejection and witchcraft had been served to this baby every day in the amniotic fluid. This could have provided ground for Satan to move in. A plan formed in my mind.

During the announcements I whispered to Barbara, "Yes, Barbara, it's very possible that Katie has a demon, but Jesus came to undo the works of the devil,[2] and church is the best place to drive any devil out of her. I'm sure our minister, Dr. Christian, would pray for her if we ask him. After the service, when Katie has sat under the preaching, let's get Bob, Katie and Dr. Christian to go into the church parlor with us and ask several other believers to pray for Katie, too. Now let's use the rest of this hour to pray, and see what God will do."

The service over, Barbara filled Bob and the girls in on the plan. Bob asked Heather to stay with the twins in the nursery until he came for them. Dr. Christian readily agreed to pray for Katie, and we asked three or four other believers to join us in the parlor. Soon our little band was assembled, holding hands in a circle with Katie in the center, looking to Dr. Christian for leadership.

"I've never tried to cast out a demon," he began, "but I know the gospels have many accounts of this, and I know that Jesus is *'the same yesterday and today and forever'* (Hebrews 13:8). He is still our strong Deliverer. Katie, we would like to pray for you. Do you agree?" When she nodded in agreement, he prayed and we waited.

Ground Level Christianity

The silence was broken by the firm bass voice of, Talbot, one of the elders. He was praying a strong prayer in Jesus' Name, commanding the devil to come out of Katie. With authority he prayed release for her in the Name of Jesus.

Prickles ran up and down my legs, and I felt hot as I sometimes do in the presence of the Holy Spirit. Had we done all we could do? Should we just say "Amen" and go in faith? Was there something for Katie to do? I realized that Katie had to confess her sin and ask forgiveness for her wicked behavior. But how? And what else should we say? What was common ground for all of us?

"Let's all pray the Lord's prayer," I said. So we began: *Our Father, who art in Heaven, hallowed be Thy name. Thy kingdom come.* "Right here, right now, Lord!" I added privately.

Thy will be done. "You came to set the captive free, Jesus!"

On earth as it is in Heaven. Give us this day our daily bread. "Deliverance is the children's bread, Lord."

And forgive us our trespasses. "Yes, Lord! She is saying it!"

As we forgive those who trespass against us. "She was forgiving her father for deserting her and her mother for dabbling in the occult!"

And lead us not into temptation, but deliver us from evil ...

"Stop!" I interjected. "Katie, honey, ask Jesus to deliver you from this evil."

She responded, "Dear Jesus, please deliver me from this evil."

Yes! It was done!

Our voices swelled in triumph: *For Thine is the kingdom, and the power, and the glory forever. Amen!*

We praised the Lord and rejoiced and hugged Katie and embraced one another and praised some more, because we knew it was done. Right there in the church parlor, little Katie was set free.

The family returned home to a peace and harmony they had never known before. Katie had a turnaround. She stopped lying and torturing her baby sisters. She became obedient and helpful. It was a miraculous change. Now twenty-two years old, she is a pleasure and a joy to her fam-

"They Will Drive Out Demons"

ily. She holds a job and is a responsible citizen. And she is still free.

One That Backfired on Me

Deliverance is not something that should be approached lightly. Briefly I would like to give an account of a deliverance that backfired on me.

One Friday I received an urgent call for help from an acquaintance in a nearby town. It seemed that the court was giving custody of the woman's two children to their father, and she was fighting depression. Unwilling to take on such a case alone, I called on my friend Janet to go with me. We drove the eighteen miles, praying for the mind of Christ. We met in the friend's church sanctuary, prayed the best we knew how and returned home.

On Saturday I didn't feel very well, but I usually don't say anything to my family about my feelings because I just look to God to heal me and simply pray about it. Sunday morning I was nauseated and weak, but I was determined to go with the family to early-morning communion, as was our custom.

Waves of nausea kept me from concentrating on the statements of faith and confession of sins. All that kneeling and standing while the gospel was read had me holding onto the pew in front of me for support. When the invitation came to receive the bread and wine, I was so weak I could hardly stand.

Suddenly I realized that the demon we had cast out two days before was afflicting me. I knew this was war, and my body was the battleground. My mind and spirit were clear and strong, however, and I clenched my teeth against the rolling nausea.

Silently I said, "Satan, the sacraments represent the body and blood of Jesus, provided for the cleansing of sin and wholeness in the body. I am going down to the altar to take communion if I have to crawl on my hands and knees!"

I may have looked pious as I slowly and carefully pulled

my weak body off the seat and deliberately held each pew I passed in order to keep from falling down. Maybe I looked emotional when I reached the altar. I knelt and dropped my head into my arms on the altar rail. Maybe I appeared desperate as my hand trembled when I reached for the wafer.

The pastor intoned, "The body of our Lord Jesus Christ, which was given for thee, preserve thy soul and body unto everlasting life. Take and eat this in remembrance that Christ died for thee, and feed on Him in thy heart by faith with thanksgiving."

Maybe the wine would not stay down, but I knew that the blood of Jesus cleanses from all unrighteousness, and Jesus came to set me free. I lifted my head for the cup, and sipped by faith, as the minister said, "The blood of our Lord Jesus Christ, which was shed for thee, preserve thy soul and body unto everlasting life. Drink this in remembrance that Christ's blood was shed for thee, and be thankful."

As soon as the wine went down my throat, all the weakness and nausea fled. I could feel the sparkle return to my eyes. I was set free!

Was I thankful? I could have jumped up and down right there in that staid Episcopal church!

What exactly tried to afflict me after Janet and I prayed for our friend I do not know, but what set me free was faith in the blood of Jesus, which will never lose its power.

Janet and I compared notes the next day. She had not been affected. I have been more careful since that day.

Our friend, too, had a happy ending. She sought help from Jesus, and He set her free. After suicide attempts, cirrhosis of the liver (as a result of a severe drinking problem), and several stays in Christian rehabilitation homes, she dried out, worked her way through law school (by working in her nursing profession), married a reformed alcoholic and now has a solid Christian family life.

There Are No Formulas

Jesus came to undo the works of the devil, wherever they are found. My purpose in telling Katie's story and mine is

"They Will Drive Out Demons"

not to suggest that the Lord's Prayer and Holy Communion are formulas for combatting the devil. This is spiritual warfare, and it must be waged spiritually with spiritual weapons — the weapons and gifts described earlier.

The issue at stake in spiritual warfare is people being rightly related to God and receiving the full benefit of being His children. Satan wants to block that, either with sin or deception. God has purposed that His people have salvation in every aspect of their lives.

We can see certain fundamental elements in the Lord's prayer that will help us in the battle:

Our Father: *"The Spirit Himself bears witness with our spirit that we are children of God, and if children, heirs also ... with Christ"* (Romans 8:16-17, NAS).

Hallowed be Thy Name: Looking to the Father with adoration, worship and praise puts children in right relationship with the Father to give homage and to receive blessings.

Thy will be done: Finding a scripture to cover our need assures that we are praying in the will of God. For example, *"No weapon that is formed against you shall prosper..."* (Isaiah 54:17, NAS). When we pray in this way, we may pray with confidence, knowing that what we are asking is the will of God. He hastens to perform His word (see Jeremiah 1:12). The Apostle John taught: *"And this is the confidence that we have in Him, that if we ask anything according to His will, He hears us. And if we know that He hears us, whatever we ask, we know that we have the petitions that we have asked of Him"* (1 John 5:14-15, NKJ).

Forgive us our sins: Sin must be confessed specifically to be forgiven (1 John 1:9).[3]

As we forgive those who sin against us: *"And when you stand praying, if you hold anything against anyone, forgive him, so that your Father in heaven may forgive you your sins"* (Mark 11:25).

Deliver us from evil: *"So if the Son sets you free, you will be free indeed"* (John 8:36). Whatever evil tries to afflict us, we can be assured that it was provided for in the atonement.

For thine is the kingdom and the power and the glory forever: Thus, even before we see the desired results, we praise God for who He is.

You may be led to deal with demon spirits in a totally different way. Be led of the Lord.

Deliverance from evil is provided in the atonement. Why should we suffer at the hands of the devil who is always present to steal, kill and destroy, when Jesus has come that we might have life and have it more abundantly? Jesus said that if we would obey the truth, the truth would set us free.

Endnotes: "They Will Drive Out Demons"

1. **Mark 16:17**—And these signs will accompany those who believe: In my name they will drive out demons ... .
2. **1 John 3:8**—He who does what is sinful is of the devil, because the devil has been sinning from the beginning. The reason the Son of God appeared was to destroy the devil's work.
3. **1 John 1:9**—If we confess our sins, he is faithful and just and will forgive us our sins and purify us from all unrighteousness.

Demystifying Deliverance

The following account in Matthew 15 about a demon-possessed girl helped demystify deliverance for me:

Jesus withdrew to the region of Tyre and Sidon. A Canaanite woman from that vicinity came to him, crying out, "Lord, Son of David, have mercy on me! My daughter is suffering terribly from demon-possession." Jesus did not answer a word. So his disciples came to him and urged him, "Send her away, for she keeps crying out after us."
He answered, "I was sent only to the lost sheep of Israel."
The woman came and knelt before him. "Lord, help me!" she said.

"They Will Drive Out Demons"

He replied, "It is not right to take the children's bread and toss it to their dogs."
"Yes, Lord," she said, "but even the dogs eat the crumbs that fall from their masters' table."
Then Jesus answered, "Woman, you have great faith! Your request is granted." And her daughter was healed from that very hour. Matthew 15:21-28

People in Bible times recognized demon possession or oppression for what it was and called it by its name. The Canaanite woman faced it and went to Jesus with the problem. Today we have medical terms and learned explanations which merely cloud the issue, and even many Christians simply don't know what to do when faced with demon activity. Looking at this account may give us some help.

In the first place, Jesus plainly stated that freedom from demon possession was *"the children's bread."* There are many examples of demon-possessed people being liberated in the New Testament. All the Spirit-empowered believers seemed to have set people free when the need arose (see Matthew 8:32, 9:33, 12:22, 15:28, 17:18, Mark 1:26, 34, 3:22-30, 5:9, 7:30, 9:23-25, 16:9, Luke 8:2, 9:42, 10:19, 11:14-23, 13:16, Acts 5:16, 8:7, 16:18, 19:12-13 and Ephesians 6:12).

The disciples learned by watching the Master. Here, in one of the early occurrences, they were as uncomfortable as we would be in that predicament. When Jesus was forced to address the situation, He said He was sent only to *"the lost sheep of Israel."* This woman was not a Jew and, at first, He refused her request on that ground. In her favor, however, we see that:

- She was honest about her problem.
- She knew Jesus could deliver her child of the demon.
- She went to Him over the stout objections of the disciples and persisted in her request.
- She knelt before Him and said, "Lord, help me," acknowledging Jesus as Lord.
- She realized that even a crumb of Jesus' power and love would heal her daughter, and she said so, exhibiting her faith.
- It was on the basis of her faith and not that she deserved it that Jesus healed her child. Faith always gets the job done.

Chapter 13

Cleaning House

Moving is a fact of life for most of us. American families move on the average of once every four years. Sometimes we get more than we bargained for in a home. The house may be painted, clean and looking nice, but is there something left behind — underneath that fresh coat of paint?

Friends of mine (let's call them Steve and Mary for the sake of this story), bought a spacious home in the best section of town. They painted it, made it look fresh and lovely and joyfully moved their four beautiful children into their new place. Before long, however, Mary was sitting on my couch weeping.

"My children are fighting with each other and rebellious toward their father and me. They have never been this way before. I don't understand it, and I don't know what to do ..." she trailed off. Then she began a long tale.

"After we had been in the house a while, Beth, our youngest, had bad dreams night after night. She cried out and woke Hannah. Steve and I were up several times with her every night. One morning I woke up feeling headachy and the children were cross, so I spent extra time praying. Things were more normal after that, except in a day or two the girls got colds.

"Then the quarreling broke out. They almost never fight with their brother. They have their dad's even disposition, especially Sarah. Besides, we don't allow them to be mean to each other. One day several days ago they were home from school, and it was almost unbearable. I wasn't feeling well anyway because I had hurt my back. Then Steve came home cranky and added to the problem. We tried to pray, but even that did not seem to help this time. I've been crying for three

Cleaning House

days. Anything sets me off, and I just can't help it. Look at me, I'm a mess. Will you pray with me?"

Mary could have asked many other Christians in town to pray with her, but unknown to her, I had information about her house that she needed to know. I knew the previous residents.

The former owner was a severe alcoholic, separated from her husband after years of strife, and finally deserted by all her family. She was a pitiful wretch.

Several years back she'd had a prayer meeting in her home, which I had attended. The atmosphere was so oppressive that praying there was almost impossible. All I could do was to say the name of Jesus during the whole meeting to defend myself against that eerie heaviness. It was this oppressive atmosphere that a coat of paint could cover but not cure.

Time for Some Old-Fashioned Housecleaning

After I told Mary about all this, I said, "Mary, the name of Jesus that protected me in that house is just as strong for you. Jesus has defeated the devil on the cross on our behalf, and we walk in that victory by faith, just like we receive our salvation, healing or any other spiritual gift."

After that, we talked some more about spiritual housecleaning, we prayed for her headache and for her family, and she went home, resolved to take action.

With Steve's knowledge and consent, Mary set up a time for her housecleaning. She asked a mutual friend, Edna, and me to help her with the spiritual warfare.

"Mary, you and Steve are the legal owners of this house, and you have authority here," I reminded her. "We all have authority in the name of Jesus, but the devil is a legal expert, and he knows his grounds. You must establish your scriptural ground here and stand on it to drive him off. The evil spirits of strife and who-knows-what-all were quiescent for a while after you moved in, but now that they have come out into the open, we can drive them out with spiritual weapons."

Just to be clear about our authority, our friend Edna said, "The Bible tells about the seventy sent out by Jesus who returned rejoicing, saying, *'Lord, even the demons submit to us in your name.'* Jesus replied, *'I have given you authority to trample on snakes and scorpions and to overcome all the power of the enemy; nothing will harm you'* (Luke 10:17 and 19)."

Edna turned to the admonition in Ephesians 6:11 to *"put on the full armor of God so that you can take your stand against the devil's schemes. For our struggle is not against flesh and blood, but against the rulers, against the authorities, against the spiritual forces of evil in heavenly realms."*

Although Mary already knew this, she had never thought of it in connection with her house. Resolve rang in her voice when she recalled, *"For though we live in the world, we do not wage war as the world does. The weapons we fight with are not the weapons of the world. On the contrary, they have divine power to demolish strongholds. We demolish arguments and every pretension that sets itself up against the knowledge of God, and we take captive every thought to make it obedient to Christ"* (2 Corinthians 10:3-5).

"Yes, the Word of God is one of our most powerful spiritual weapons," Edna said. "We establish our legal ground with it. Otherwise we are just praying a wish. Neither God nor the devil is obliged to heed what we say. But God is ready to perform His Word."

Putting on the Whole Armor of God

"Before we go to war, we need to put on the armor of God,"[1] Edna reminded us. "That armor is described in Ephesians 6:13 and following: The helmet of salvation (and the mind of Christ, see 1 Corinthians 2:16), the breastplate of righteousness imparted to us by faith in the blood shed by Jesus for us on the cross, the girdle of truth, the sword of the Spirit which is the Word of God in our mouths, the shield

Cleaning House

of faith held up to quench all the fiery darts of the enemy and the sandals of the Gospel of peace.

"And the blood of Jesus and the resurrection power of God," Mary added.

"Now we can get down to business, Mary," I said. "You, as the lawful owner of this house, can give permission to anyone you choose to come in here. If you want Jesus to be the Lord and ruling power in your home, you can give Him that place. You can take back your house from any demons that were here by permission of the former owners. Jesus has already defeated the devil, but we get His victory in our home by faith.

"Just like Joshua was instructed to do with the Promised Land,[2] you do with your home. Fight! God promised the land to the children of Israel, but they had to take it by conquest. This is war.

"Start with Joshua 1:3, where God says: *'Every place that the sole of your foot will tread upon I have given you,'* and let's go."

Taking Possession

So our little army followed Mary, holding the Bible which was opened to Joshua. Across the room, down the hall and into every room in the house — closets, bathrooms and pantry included — we went. We went "upstairs, downstairs and in my lady's chamber" — into every nook and cranny.

Mary said loudly, "Every place my foot treads I claim for the glory of God, according to the Scriptures. I have authority here in the mighty name of Jesus, and I give that authority to Almighty God to rule and reign over this family and this house. Jesus is Lord here. The blood of Jesus cleanses this house of all unrighteousness. In the name of Jesus, I command all evil spirits to leave this house."

First one and then another spoke to the principalities, powers and wicked spirits of the air,[3] obeying the scriptural admonition *"casting down ... every high thing that exalts itself against the knowledge of God, bringing every thought into captivity to the obedience of Christ"* (2 Corinthians 10:5).

As we performed the spiritual housecleaning, we were sensitive to the leading of the Holy Spirit. When we were satisfied we had done everything we could do, we ended by singing triumphantly:

> *God's got an army marching through this land*
> *Deliverance in their song, and healing in their hand,*
> *Everlasting joy and gladness in their heart,*
> *In this army I've got a part!*

A happy Mary greeted her children as they came home from school that day. She told them what had been the matter with their family since their move into the new home. They prayed together, declaring that Jesus was the Lord of their lives and their home and bringing all those *"thoughts and imaginations, and every high thing that exalts itself against the knowledge of God into obedience to Christ."* There was wonderful peace ... for a time.

Several weeks later Mary was on my sofa again, crying. "Everything was so much better, Janice, after you and Edna and I cleaned house. The children were their own sweet selves, and I didn't have headaches. But look at me now. I'm a mess again. It's so bad that Steve and I are arguing over the children — something we have never done. Does the house need 'cleaning' again?

"Something happened about a week ago that upset me, and I don't know why. Do you think this might have something to do with the same problem?" And she began an unusual story.

Identifying Invaders

"Last week a client of Steve's came to the door after supper. We invited him in and soon discovered that he was not there to discuss business, but to let us in on a wonderful opportunity. Since he liked Steve, he wanted to show him

Cleaning House

how he could increase his business, help his employees and influence the people around him. He said something about 'mind control,' or the like ... Have you ever heard of anything like that?" she asked. I nodded yes, so she went on.

"We told him that we always pray about business decisions and employee problems. We depend on Jesus for our guidance. We asked him if he knew Jesus, and he said the strangest thing. He said, 'Oh, yes, we believe in Jesus. He is one of our main controls.' It wasn't clear what he meant, but whenever I tried to bring in scripture, he took the conversation in another direction.

"He walked around in the house and touched the walls and said 'Oh, there's a hollow place here ...' and strange things like that. Then he went outside and walked around the house in the garden, looking up at the moon and saying, 'It's a good night for spiritual activity, isn't it?'

"Finally Steve called attention to the late hour and actually asked the man to leave. When we got the children settled in bed, we went into the breakfast room where my Bible was open. I started to read a passage out loud and, for some strange reason, terror struck me. I was speechless, unable to read or call out, hardly able to stand. I have never been so struck down by fear. I could hardly breathe. I looked at Steve, and he was immobilized too. It was marrow-melting, stomach-cramping terror! We gaped at each other, paralyzed and pinned to the floor with invisible chains.

Paralyzing Terror

" 'Jesus, Jesus, Jesus ...' in a whisper was all I could get out. Steve just stood rooted to the floor of the breakfast room, which moments before had seemed so safe. Now fear was so thick in there we couldn't battle it away.

" 'Jesus, Jesus, Jesus ...' came out stronger. I looked to Steve for help, but he was as paralyzed as I.

"Then Steve joined in, 'Jesus ... Jesus ... Jesus ... '

"Almost as suddenly as it had come, the thick fright

evaporated, and once again we could move and talk a little. But ever since I've had these unpredictable attacks of fear.

"Am I crazy to connect this with the confusion in our household? Why didn't our housecleaning 'stick'?" she finished.

"I don't know," I answered. "Let's pray about it and see if God will enlighten us." After prayer I asked, "Mary, did you tell Steve all about the housecleaning?"

"Certainly!" she replied. "We talk about everything."

"What was his reaction? Did he understand?"

"Yes. He had never heard of doing that, but he knew the scriptures, and he was glad that we did it."

"Mary, maybe everyone in the family needs to be involved in the housecleaning this time. Maybe there was someplace where we failed to clean out all the former resident's evil spirits, like the attic or the basement. When that man came into your home, bringing those mind control spirits, it may have brought them out of hiding. Or maybe he brought them with him.

"Would Steve participate in the housecleaning? He can learn to exercise his authority under Jesus to protect his own home and family. He'll be a wonderful warrior."

Then I told her about my six-foot-six friend, Bob, who cleaned out his two-hundred-year-old house of two hundred years' worth of demons, while his wife, Barbara and the children, Heather, Katie and the twins, trailed around behind him saying, "Jesus is Lord." And Jesus took over from all the evil accumulated in the past two hundred years.

Overpowering the Devil

The next time Mary came, there was jubilant victory to report. "Steve took that scripture and his authority under Jesus and really routed the devil," she said. "At first the things he did seemed kind of rote and maybe an exercise in futility. Maybe he was just going over the same territory we had already covered, but when he went into the attic, he said the hair on his head stood straight up. He was sure there

Cleaning House

were demons there. He's got a pretty loud voice when he wants to raise it, and we thought he was trying to raise the roof! He stood his ground until they left.

"When he came down, he asked me, 'Did you clean out the basement?' and I remembered that we hadn't. When he headed down there, he had 'blood in his eye.' This was war, and it was real!

"At first, all the children and I could hear was Steve's voice proclaiming 'Jesus is Lord' in the basement. Then, do you know, we could hear sounds like something beating on the pipes down there! We prayed, using faith to cover Steve with the blood of Jesus and the full armor of God, singing the victory. Praise God, we are all one in Christ in this family!

"When Steve came up those basement steps, he looked dazed. 'If I didn't believe in evil spirits before, I do now,' he said. 'Did you hear those pipes? It sounded as if someone was rattling them when I told the demons to leave in the name of Jesus. I was too busy to be afraid, but it crossed my mind. I just stood my ground and spoke to those principalities and powers and wicked spirits. I told them that Jesus is Lord in this place. He has defeated Satan on the cross and given me the victory. They have to clear out because I give this place to Almighty God, just like I gave myself to Him when I was born again.'

"Wow! The children were excited and proud of their dad. This was better than anything on TV.

"We had to let off steam, so we just burst out singing God's praise."

Certainly this is an extreme example of housecleaning. I could recount many less dramatic experiences, and I expect most housecleanings would be less wild than this one. But the principles are the same for anyone who moves into a house occupied by another family's baggage. Once entrenched, evil spirits like to hang around where they are already in control.

We can think about our lives in the same way. We can claim every single part, from the attic (our thoughts and feelings) to the basement (our family inheritance and traditions), and all around (our physical bodies) for Christ alone. Jesus will cleanse every part of us, routing out every influence the enemy has ever had on us. Call it a personal housecleaning.

Our Supernatural Weapons

Since we can't see wicked spirits and powers of the air, we must sense their presence by the Spirit and deal with them with the spiritual weapons provided for us in the Scriptures. These weapons are not like the world's, but they are *"mighty"* (2 Corinthians 10:4-5, KJV). God has provided the weapons we need to *"pull down"* these strongholds and live in peace. Some of these weapons are: discernment of spirits, faith, the Scriptures, the blood of Jesus, the name of Jesus and the full armor of God.

No matter who lived in your house before you arrived, when you come in, if you are a believer, you bring the Holy Spirit with you. Jesus, our Forerunner, has made the way for us to be *"more than conquerors through him who loved us"* (Romans 8:37). We don't battle against flesh and blood, but against wicked spirits in high places. But our mighty weapons through God can demolish strongholds when we use them. The Lord has promised: " *'No weapon formed against you will prevail, and you will refute every tongue that accuses you. This is the heritage of the servants of the Lord, and this is their vindication from me' declares the Lord"* (Isaiah 54:17).

From all this, we can conclude that the evil spirits need hold no terror for us because we know our responsibility and God's power. This is *Ground Level Christianity* — right in the house where we live.

Endnotes: Cleaning House

1. **2 Corinthians 10:4-5**—The weapons we fight with are not the weapons of the world. On the contrary, they have divine power to demolish strongholds. We demolish arguments and every pretension that sets itself up against the knowledge of God, and we take captive every thought to make it obedient to Christ.

Cleaning House

2. **Joshua 1**
3. **Ephesians 6:12**—For our struggle is not against flesh and blood, but against the rulers, against the authorities, against the powers of this dark world and against the spiritual forces of evil in the heavenly realms.

More On Spiritual Housecleaning

Why can we expect to drive out demons if they are in possession of the territory? Joshua was the model for us. God said that he would take the land back from the Canaanites who were occupying it: *"Do not be terrified by them, for the LORD your God, who is among you, is a great and awesome God. The LORD your God will drive out those nations before you, little by little. You will not be allowed to eliminate them all at once, or the wild animals will multiply around you. But the LORD your God will deliver them over to you, throwing them into great confusion until they are destroyed. He will give their kings into your hand, and you will wipe out their names from under heaven. No one will be able to stand up against you; you will destroy them"* (Deuteronomy 7:21-24).

This is so because *"the one [Jesus] who is in you is greater than he [the devil] who is in the world [or the house]"* (1 John 4:4). John said the reason the Son of God appeared was *"to destroy the devil's work"* (1 John 3:8). One translation says, *"undoing the works of the devil"* [PHIL]. *"If God is for us, who can be against us?"* (Romans 8:31). *"No, in all these things we are more than conquerors through him who loved us"* (Romans 8:37).

When we come into a place, we bring Jesus with us. We have the Holy Spirit, the power of the blood of Jesus, the resurrection power and the authority of Almighty God! The light has come and the darkness cannot put it out, or even understand it (see John 1:5).

We stand clothed in the full armor of God (see Ephesians 6:10), in the authority of Almighty God. In the mighty name of Jesus, we can drive out devils and wicked spirits in high places and possess the land for the glory of God!

The Apostle Paul wrote: *"Finally, be strong in the Lord and in*

Ground Level Christianity

his mighty power. Put on the full armor of God so that you can take your stand against the devil's schemes. For our struggle is not against flesh and blood, but against the rulers, against the authorities, against the powers of this dark world and against the spiritual forces of evil in the heavenly realms. Therefore put on the full armor of God, so that when the day of evil comes, you may be able to stand your ground, and after you have done everything, to stand. Stand firm then, with the belt of truth buckled around your waist, with the breastplate of righteousness in place, and with your feet fitted with the readiness that comes from the gospel of peace. In addition to all this take up the shield of faith, with which you can extinguish all the flaming arrows of the evil one. Take the helmet of salvation and the sword of the Spirit, which is the word of God" (Ephesians 6:10-17).

Chapter 14

High-Stakes Fasting

Nowadays, fasting, or abstaining from food, is mostly for people trying to lose weight. Fasting as a spiritual discipline, however, is found in both the Old and New Testaments of the Bible. In the gospels we see Jesus fasting and teaching His disciples to fast. Jesus fasted forty days before His temptation by Satan, like Moses did on Mt. Sinai before God gave the Ten Commandments. In Acts we see Cornelius, the Roman centurion, fasting before Peter comes to his house, where salvation and the baptism of the Holy Spirit were extended to the Gentiles. In Antioch we see the new believers gathered to fast before the Holy Spirit directed them to send out Paul and Barnabas to carry the Gospel to the Gentiles in Macedonia.

The Scriptures promise rewards for fasting. Anyone who practices fasting receives many benefits, some of which are listed below. These benefits are physical, mental, spiritual and social. Isaiah 58, which contains many of these promises, is quoted in part at the end of this chapter.

We should note concerning fasting:
- It was part of the Law given by God (see Leviticus 23:27).
- It sharpens spiritual sensitivity (see Acts 13:1-11).
- It helps keep the body under subjection to the Spirit (see 1 Corinthians 9:27).
- It humbles the one who fasts (see Psalm 35:13) so that God can exalt him in due time (Luke 14:11, 18:14 and 1 Peter 5:6).
- It changes events (2 Chronicles 20, Esther 4:16 and Jonah 3:5-10).
- It gives evidence of repentance and improves relation-

ships with God and man (Nehemiah 9, Joel 2:15 and Jonah 3:5).
- Jesus fasted (Matthew 4:2 and Matthew 6:16). So did Moses, David, Elijah, Daniel, Isaiah, Paul and most of the other heroes of the Bible (see Exodus 24:18, 34:28, Deuteronomy 9:9, 18, 2 Samuel 12:16, 1 Kings 19:8, Acts 14:23 and Daniel 9:3).

Why, then do we hear so little about fasting?

Shaping History through Fasting

One book on fasting, *Shaping History By Prayer and Fasting* by Derek Prince, so intrigued me that I thought I would try fasting. I might not try to shape history, but I certainly needed to pray more effectively for my town, my state, my nation and the world. So I began fasting on the day the prayer group met at our home. We were no longer contented with business-as-usual at prayer meeting. We wanted to see some action. We said, "Here, Father, we're available. You might want to do things we've not seen before." And things began to happen!

A little boy was healed of blindness. He had looked directly at the sun during an eclipse, even though he had been warned that it would burn his retina if he did. A woman was healed of deafness, although doctors at Duke University Hospital had given her no hope that she could hear again without aid. Eight cases of cystitis were healed in one meeting. Smoking addiction was broken. The prayer-group members, while not free of problems, began to have more joy and peace.

Fasting is not to twist God's arm or to impress Him with our sincerity. Fasting makes us stronger spiritually. It keeps our spiritual life on track. Periodic fasting, like regular worship, provides a rhythm and tempo to life that factors God in consistently. Fasting is also the big gun for big spiritual battles (see Matthew 4, Mark 1 and Luke 4).[1]

High-Stakes Fasting
A Big Battle

Parenting is a big responsibility, and occasionally it seems like a battleground. Sometimes in child rearing, persuasion won't do the job, punishment causes resentment and confrontation brings outright rebellion. What's a parent to do? Bring out the big guns for the big battle.

One summer, while we were in the mountains, one of our girls was acting rather sullen and uncommunicative. She didn't help around the house and mostly stayed away. One day she borrowed my car, brought it back caked in mud and went off to play with friends instead of cleaning it up. She stayed out so late I called the security officer in our community to ask if there had been any reports of accidents. Perhaps this might be a profile of any teenager at one time or another, but a pattern was developing that would make neither of us very happy if it continued. Worst of all, her behavior was totally out of character for a child of God.

Persuasion didn't help. She was deaf to reasoning. Punishment turned her into a petulant martyr. I stopped short of confrontation. Instead I brought out the big guns for the big battle.

There was so much more at stake here than just mother-daughter relations or a storm that would "just blow over." It seemed that this child's life was taking a wrong direction. This was bigger than both of us, but not too big for God. I was not fighting mere flesh and blood in this case, but wicked spirits in high places were after my daughter (see Ephesians 6:10-12). I needed to bring out the weapons with divine power to demolish strongholds and arguments that set themselves up against the knowledge of God (see 2 Corinthians 10:4-5). I was led to roll out the Big Fast.

I arranged to go to a church camp in Virginia for three days of prayer and fasting. Being at camp was such a satisfying experience for me that I didn't feel that I was making a great sacrifice by not eating. On the contrary, I had a wonderful time basking in the presence of the Lord and enjoying the company of like-minded people. I didn't talk about my problem or even ask for prayer. I used mealtime to pray. Including a day's travel up and a day's travel back, I fasted five days.

Back home we were all glad to be reunited, and the next day my daughter built a fire against the cool, rainy day. We sat in two rocking chairs gazing at the flames, and I couldn't help but notice a sweet peace between us. Almost as a discovery, I commented to her, "You know, Honey, it wasn't mother you were rebelling against. It was God. I was just the most convenient object to push against."

The daughter who heard those words wasn't the daughter I'd left five days earlier. God had done a work in her, gently wooing her back onto the right path again. Once more she seemed relieved that someone else knew her secret and could put it into words. She said slowly, " *'And rebellion is as the sin of witchcraft,'* " quoting from Samuel's statement to King Saul when he disobeyed God.[2]

When the Holy Spirit convicts us of sin, it may hurt, but not as much as it helps, because He also shows us the way out of the problem. The love of God washed over our hearts as the fire warmed our souls. Then my daughter took the next step. To restore her fellowship with God and with her mother, she confessed the sin, repented and asked forgiveness. The large living room was almost not big enough to hold that holy moment.

Now, in retrospect, I see a principle at work which Jesus summarized in the Sermon on the Mount: *"Seek first the kingdom of God and His righteousness, and all these things shall be added to you"* (Matthew 6:33, NKJ). Hadn't I learned this before on the golf course?

Surprising Dos and Don'ts

There is a whole chapter in the Bible on fasting: Isaiah 58. In it God speaks to hypocritical people who obey the letter of the Law on fasting instead of engaging in the struggle for the good of the people around them. Fasting needs to be matched with obedience. In this chapter, God says through Isaiah: *"The kind of fast I want is that you stop oppressing those*

High-Stakes Fasting

who work for you and treat them fairly and give them what they earn. I want you to share your food with the hungry and bring right into your own homes those who are helpless, poor and destitute. Clothe those who are cold and don't hide from relatives who need your help.

"If you do these things, God will shed his own glorious light upon you. He will heal you; your godliness will lead you forward, and goodness will be a shield before you, and the glory of the Lord will protect you from behind. Then, when you call, the Lord will answer. 'Yes, I am here,' he will quickly reply. All you need to do is stop oppressing the weak, and to stop making false accusations and spreading vicious rumors!

"Feed the hungry! Help those in trouble! Then your light will shine out from the darkness, and the darkness around you shall be as bright as day. And the Lord will guide you continually, and satisfy you with all good things, and keep you healthy, too; and you will be like a well-watered garden, like an ever-flowing spring" (Isaiah 58:6-11, TLB).

My conclusion is that if we do these things *and* fast, we will please God and follow Jesus' example too. He did it to prepare Himself for tests that were ahead. After fasting in the wilderness forty days, Jesus had to face the devil's temptations. He also fasted before He chose His disciples. Jesus told them: *"And now about fasting. When you fast, declining your food for a spiritual purpose, don't do it publicly .... But when you fast, put on festive clothing so that no one will suspect you are hungry, except your Father who knows every secret. And he will reward you"* (Matthew 6:16-18, TLB).

So there are rewards, as my story shows. But the Father rewards in secret, as well as openly, because He fills the empty place left by mortifying the flesh with the personality of Jesus. The stakes are high in life's tests, and fasting is a big gun for the big battles.

Endnotes: High-Stakes Fasting

1. These three gospels tell of Jesus' forty-day fast in the wilderness before He met the devil's temptations: Matthew 4:2, Mark 1:12 and Luke 4:2

2. **1 Samuel 15:22-23**—Behold, to obey is better than sacrifice, and to hearken than the fat of rams. For rebellion is as the sin of witchcraft, and stubbornness is as iniquity and idolatry (KJV).

Chapter 15

The Power of Forgiveness

My ninety-three-year-old friend Cornelia couldn't seem to die.

After a full life of service to her husband, five children and many families in town, she was weak, helpless and bedridden. She had helped me countless times with our children. Many people loved her, and her fig preserves were prized in our home.

Now, alone in her house, she needed attention that her children could not easily give, because they lived too far away. Her son Dan came frequently from Washington, D.C., to visit her and to repair her house. He tried to see that she had the care she needed.

Dan was there when I went to visit Cornelia, bringing food and a leather-bound, large-print New Testament for her. She accepted the food and carefully unwrapped the book, which clearly meant more to her than the food.

In a quiet voice she pointed out a condiment set up in the cupboard. "I want you to have it. To remember me. So I'll know that someone has it that knows ... ," she didn't finish. I tried to tell her that I couldn't take her gift, but she insisted. She lapsed into a tired silence, closing her eyes. No arguments. So I tiptoed out her door into the living room.

Dan was pacing in the living room, talking wildly to himself, uttering vituperations on an alcoholic breath. The living room was just wide enough to hold a horsehair sofa on the side opposite the doorway to Cornelia's room. Next to her doorway were a couple of chairs and a table. The walkway between led to the kitchen and was carpeted with a worn Victorian flower patterned carpet. The room was dimly illuminated by light filtering through a faintly colored stained glass window above the sofa.

When I told him what Cornelia had said about the condiment set, it triggered a tirade — not at me but about his four sisters: how they were just waiting for their mother to die to get her money, how there wasn't enough money to pay for nursing care, how he had to stay here with her because they wouldn't, how the house was standing and in good shape only because he'd fixed it and paid for the repairs, how it should rightfully go to him, how the nieces he'd hired with his own money didn't look after Cornelia, how it had all fallen on him ...

The emotions just boiled over. The best thing I could do was to listen to him. No one else would. I hated to hear all the family problems, so I began to pray and listen to God.

"Wait," God seemed to be saying. "When he runs down, ask him if things are so unbearable that he would be willing to give them to Me."

After the second round of the same complaints, Dan suddenly realized that he'd said it all before. Nobody was arguing or disagreeing. He hung his head over drooping shoulders under the weight of it all. With resistance gone, I asked him God's question.

Poof! The air went out of him like a spent balloon. He gaped at me a minute while the silence pressed my question.

"Well, I guess so," he mumbled. "How?"

I eased off the sofa onto my knees.

"We'll ask God," I said, hoping he would kneel beside me.

Dan knelt beside me, and things began to change.

"We'll pray something like this: 'Dear God, I can't stand this anymore. This is too much for me to carry. Please take it. I give it to You.' Can you say something like that?"

"I guess I can." So we did.

"Now, Dan, will you give yourself to God? He loves you. He sees all the good you have tried to do, as well as all the bad, and He loves you. He can take care of you and your

The Power of Forgiveness

problems better than you can. And He wants to. He loves you. He loves Cornelia, and He can take care of her, too. Let's do that, okay?"

"Okay."

"Dan," I said, "ask God to take control of your life. Ask Jesus to be your Lord and Savior, to forgive you of your sins and let you live for Him from now on. In your own words, in your own way."

"Okay." And he began to weep as he spoke his surrender into the sofa.

After a silence, we prayed the Lord's Prayer through the line that says *"forgive us our debts as we forgive our debtors,"* and there we stopped.

"Dan, you want God to forgive you of your sins completely, but Jesus taught that He can forgive us only as we forgive others. You have just told me about all the things you've got against all these people ... ."

"They didn't ask me to forgive them," he replied. "They're not sorry. They keep on doing those things. How can I forgive them? They don't deserve it."

"Forgiveness is a decision, Dan, not an emotion. We forgive because God tells us to do it, like we just prayed. You have just asked Jesus to be your Lord and to forgive your sins, so when He asks you to forgive others you have to do it. Like this: 'Dear Lord, I forgive Ada for everything she has ever done against me, or against Mama, and for all the things I've ever thought she has done — whether she really did them or not.' "

One by one he forgave his sisters, his nieces and everyone he'd held something against. It came easier and easier.

When Dan's face came up out of the sofa, he filled his lungs with new air. He looked at me with shining eyes, aglow with love. He had a new Lord and a new life. His load of resentment was gone.

And then we concluded the prayer: *"For Thine is the kingdom and the power and the glory forever! Amen! Hallelujah!"*

That night the call came that Cornelia had died and gone to Heaven. By midday the next day many of her descendants

Ground Level Christianity

and relatives had gathered from near and far. To help with meals I took Brunswick stew. At my knock the front door opened to reveal two lines of people seated in the dim living room, and they nodded in a guarded way as I passed into the kitchen.

The kitchen was light and airy, and fresh flowers were on the table, where people were putting food.

As I left the kitchen, the front door burst open and Dan galloped into the room, shouting, "I'm a new man! I've been saved! I'm a new man!" He almost danced with excitement.

"Jesus loves me! I love everybody! Jesus loves everybody! Jesus loves you, too. I'm a new man. I've been saved! Jesus wants to save you, too!"

Dan? This was not the Dan they knew! He was on fire for the Lord, not all fired up with "likker"! Dan woke up the wake with the light of the Jesus.

The changes in Dan's life have been lasting. Today Dan tells everybody he sees about Jesus and the power He has to save, forgive and heal. He brings light into all the dark places of life. People of all races call Dan to pray for their sick. He carries in his pocket many letters of thanks and testimonies to the healing power of his prayers.

For twenty years Dan has been telling people what it meant to him when he forgave everyone everything they had ever done to hurt him, or things he thought they had done against him. After he made the decision to forgive, God made the forgiveness real to him. Then he asked God to forgive him of his own sins, and God made that real in his heart, too.

Dan read in Cornelia's Bible what Jesus taught about forgiveness:

- When you stand praying, forgive, or your heavenly Father will not forgive you (see Matthew 6:14).
- God forgives us exactly like we forgive others — partially, fully or not at all (see Matthew 6:14-15).
- Don't take communion if you have anything against your brother (see 1 Corinthians 11:27-32).

The Power of Forgiveness

- Don't even present a gift to God until you are reconciled with your brother (see Matthew 5:23-24).
- If a brother sins against you, Jesus said to forgive him up to four hundred and ninety times if necessary (see Matthew 18:22-23).
- Our Heavenly Father will deliver us to the torturers if we do not forgive from our heart a brother who trespasses against us (see Matthew 18:32-35).

Dan had been in the hands of the torturers until he forgave from his heart all the offenses, real or imagined. He didn't think those people deserved forgiveness when they hadn't said they were sorry or asked to be forgiven, but after he had obeyed the command to forgive, he could see that this is exactly what Jesus did. When the soldiers crucified Him, Jesus said, *"Father, forgive them, for they do not know what they are doing"* (Luke 23:34). He forgave all of us before we asked, too.

Now, when I see Cornelia's condiment set on the shelf, it reminds me of her and Dan and the transforming power of forgiveness.

Chapter 16

Tithing

Tithing sets the record straight — Who owns and who owes. Bringing tithes into the temple of God is an act of worship, a statement that:

All things come of thee, [O Lord].
And of thine own have we given thee.
  1 Chronicles 29:14, KJV

Tithing shows the heart attitude. Like baptism, it's an "outward symbol of an inward grace."

How can anyone get his heart right enough to give to God? Especially when he can't make his income meet the basic requirements of food, clothing and shelter as it is? A dollar at a time. At least that is the way it was for Libby.

Libby was a young wife and mother of two small children. She had very little education, having stayed home from school several days every week to look after her four younger brothers and sisters while their mother worked. Their father was away. By ninth grade she had dropped out of school completely. Soon she married, had a baby and divorced. Now in her second marriage and with her second child, her life was in chaos.

The mental health clinic was just down the street from our home, so Libby stopped in for prayer group that met there after her weekly visit to her psychiatrist. She was a born-again, Spirit-filled believer, but she was quite literally walking both sides of the street — the clinical side and the faith side.

One day our prayer group was studying the few references to tithing there are in the Bible. From Abraham to

Tithing

Moses, Isaiah to Malachi, God is very clear about returning the first fruits to the Temple: *"Will a man rob God? Surely not! And yet you have robbed me.*

" 'What do you mean? When did we ever rob you?'

"You have robbed me of the tithes and offerings due to me. And so the awesome curse of God is cursing you .... Bring all the tithes into the storehouse so that there will be food enough in my Temple; if you do, I will open up the windows of heaven for you and pour out a blessing so great you won't have room enough to take it in!

"Try it! Let me prove it to you! Your crops will be large, for I will guard them from insects and plagues. Your grapes won't shrivel away before they ripen," says the Lord Almighty. "And all the nations will call you blessed, for you will be a land sparkling with happiness. These are the promises of the Lord Almighty" (Malachi 3:8-12, TLB).

New Testament references to tithing are few but clear: *"Now here are the directions about the money you are collecting to send to the Christians in Jerusalem .... On every Lord's Day each of you should put aside something from what you have earned during the week, and use it for this offering. The amount depends upon how much the Lord has helped you earn"* (1 Corinthians 16:1-2, TLB).

Libby seemed resentful of a God who would take her last nickel. But Libby is different from most of us. She takes God literally. Her shorthand credo is: God said it, I believe it and that settles it!

Libby went home to pray about what she had learned about tithing. She liked God's promises to those who tithe, and she couldn't be much worse off if she tried it. So during the Wednesday night church service she put in a crumpled dollar bill — her last. She put it in believing for a tenfold return.[1]

That Friday I opened the door to a breathless Libby. "Look, look!" she shrilled as she counted out on my kitchen table ten tattered one-dollar bills. "Look what the Lord has done! I got four dollars for baby-sitting and seven dollars for cleaning my mother-in-law's house! I used a dollar for gas and have ten to give to the Lord!" she ended triumphantly. She couldn't wait to give to God.

And she did give. Clothes that didn't fit she gave to others on the farm. She gave her winter coat to a lady who didn't have one. If Libby saw a vagrant on her country road, she invited him in for a meal, sat him down and prayed with him — just as if he were Jesus. All the while God was prospering Libby's husband in his job as a farm equipment salesman.

How do you tithe if you don't go to church? Libby asked herself. So the family began going to church on Sundays and Wednesdays. Libby and her family found that regular church attendance encouraged not only tithing, but also "Sunday clothes" and a routine that brought order and rhythm into their chaotic family life.

Libby began to tithe her time. She gave the first part of the day to studying the Bible with a dictionary beside her notebook and pen. God began to multiply her meager education into mastery of His Word.

One day Libby announced to prayer group: "I'm never going to say 'I'm frustrated' again! All the times I've said it I've put a curse on myself! Never again! I've asked God to forgive me. Just look at what the dictionary says about frustration: 'to disappoint, deceive, trick, to bring to nothing... counteract, baffle, defeat; rendering worthless of efforts directed to some end; thwart, blocking a person or thing so as to discourage further efforts; to baffle by confusion or bewildering; ... to balk by setting up obstacles or obstructions... .'

"Never again! I won't help Satan with my mouth!"

From then till now, Satan can't foil, baffle, defeat or render worthless Libby's family's efforts directed to the end of honoring God by tithing their time, talents and money to the Lord. Libby has seen her husband come to faith in Jesus Christ and eventually serve as superintendent of the Sunday school. Now there are four children, all one in Christ, attending Christian schools. Libby served as secretary of the Parents' Organization and put herself through nurse's train-

Tithing

ing in the Community College. God has prospered them in every area of their lives.

As a declaration of Libby's independence from poverty and chaos, and in recognition of her newness of life in Christ, she has changed her name. "My name is Liberty now. Please call me by my name," she announced in prayer group one day.

"How many people do you know," Liberty asked me on her birthday, "that by the time they are forty years old have four healthy children and live in their own paid-for home debt free? Considering where we've come from, that I've been a stay-home mother caring for my children and that my husband is 'only a salesman,' you know it had to be God!"

Liberty explains tithing like this: "It's a little like our backyard well, with the hand pump that brings the water up. There is plenty of water down there, but we have to prime the pump first before we can get the water to flow up the stem. First, we have to pour water down into the well before any water will come up — no matter how hard we pump the handle up and down at the top. Unless we start it by putting water into it, we can't draw any water out. Tithing is priming the pump.

"Tithing is like praising God, too. Look what the Living Bible says in Psalm 92: *'It is good to say "Thank you" to the Lord, to sing praises to the God who is above all gods. Every morning tell him, "Thank you for your kindness," and every evening rejoice in all his faithfulness. Sing his praises ... . You have done so much for me, O Lord. No wonder I am glad! I sing for joy'* (Psalm 92:1-4, TLB).

"Again, it's a little like priming the pump. We pour in praises, and we draw out God."

Tithing sets the record straight. God owns it all. When we tithe, we admit our dependence on Him. God wants to open the windows of Heaven to us and give it all to us — blessings so enormous we can't hold them all. He has given us the keys to the bank. He wants us to be sparkling with happiness. Let's do it His way.[2]

Ground Level Christianity

God is such a personal God that each one's experience with tithing is unique. In my case, I had to meet all the expenses for the children and myself on a fixed allowance when my husband was gone for months at a time on business. I couldn't make the money go around. One day I was writing checks in my big ledger checkbook and coming up short — again. I put my head down on my arms and all but cried: "Oh, God, if I give You the first ten percent, will You please manage the other ninety? I can't do it." From then on He has managed the whole amount, but He changed my priorities along the way.

To me, the most significant rewards of tithing are not necessarily monetary, although it's easier to keep score with dollars than with spiritual blessings. To me, the greatest benefit of tithing is in relationship with God, affirming my dependence upon Him for everything. The most precious boon has come when God brought all my children and grandchildren into His Kingdom and moved them all back to their hometown.[3] But first I had to give them up to God — just like tithing.

All things come of thee, [O Lord],
And of thine own have we given thee.

Endnotes: Tithing

1. **Mark 4:8**—Still other seed fell on good soil. It came up, grew and produced a crop, multiplying thirty, sixty, or even a hundred times.
2. **2 Corinthians 9:6-7**—Remember this: Whoever sows sparingly will reap sparingly, and whoever sows generously will also reap generously. Each man should give what he has decided in his heart to give, not reluctantly or under compulsion, for God loves a cheerful giver.
3. **Malachi 3:11**—And I will rebuke the devourer for your sakes, and he shall not destroy the fruits of your ground (KJV).

Everything connects man with his Creator in the Bible. Can you catch the philosophy behind these psalms?

Tithing

Psalm 39:12—I am your guest. I am a traveler passing through the earth, as all my fathers were (TLB).

Psalm 39:4 and 6—Help me to realize how brief my time on earth will be ... and all [my] busy rushing ends in nothing. [A man] heaps up riches for someone else to spend (TLB).

Psalm 40:6—It isn't sacrifices and offerings you really want from your people ... . But you have accepted the offering of my life-long service (TLB).

Chapter 17

The Power of Persistence in Prayer

Jesus tells a story of a woman who badgered an unjust judge until he granted her justice. Jesus said: *"And will not God bring about justice for his chosen ones, who cry out to him day and night? Will he keep putting them off? I tell you, he will see that they get justice, and quickly"* (Luke 18:7-8).

I cried out to God day after day for nine months to find a shipment of furniture that was lost between China and the USA, only I called it persistence in prayer. God rewarded both the woman in Jesus' story and me, and the proof is sitting in my living room.

My story began in Hong Kong, where I found a skilled Chinese furniture maker whose work I liked. Patrick Tan said he could make me two hand-carved cedar chests and two rosewood garden stools and send them to my home in Rocky Mount. He knew exactly where we live because he made furniture for Boone's Antiques in Wilson, North Carolina, eighteen miles away.

Our daughters are musicians and they had accumulated lots of music and needed chests to hold it. Their great-grandmother and grandmother had beautiful chests from China, and the girls had always loved them, so here was a way to fill two needs.

Patrick suggested that since the chests would be empty, I might want him to put in them all the souvenirs I had collected on the mainland of China during the past month. He could send everything together on a container ship. So I thanked him and left all my treasures with him to be shipped in his container. There were beautiful linens, cloisonné vases, hand-carved ink stands, backward books of Chinese seals, fans, jewelry, handkerchiefs, silk handbags, Christmas tree

The Power of Persistence in Prayer

ornaments and more. I had done all my Christmas shopping in China. I flew home, light as a feather, and pleased with the arrangement. It was August of 1984.

Two months later, in October, the shipping company, U.S. Lines, called from Norfolk to tell me that the shipment had landed in Oakland, California. They would send my treasures overland to the customs office in Norfolk, where I could pay the duty on the shipment and pick it up when it arrived. *Plenty of time until Christmas, so I can have gifts for everybody on my list*, I thought.

Another month passed, and nothing had arrived. I called the U.S. Lines' office. The secretary, Beverly Craft, assured me that she would call me as soon as she had news. Two more weeks passed and no news. In December, still nothing. Finally Beverly said they expected the boxes to arrive on January 3.

Christmas shopping that year was no fun. I was so disappointed about my furniture shipment with all the gifts not arriving in time.

They didn't come in January either.

In February, I began to pray in earnest: "Dear Heavenly Father, Your Word says that Your eyes range throughout the earth to strengthen those whose hearts are fully committed to You (see 2 Chronicles 16:9). My heart isn't perfect, but I'm confessed up to date, and I have faith that You will do what Your Word says. You know where those boxes are. Please bring them to me. In Jesus' Name. Thank you, Father."

I prayed with our prayer group, my family, the church and everybody else I could think of who knew how to pray, asking God to bring them to me. In the meantime I called Hong Kong to talk to Patrick Tan. I prayed with the furniture maker, with Beverly Craft and with another clerk in the office of the shipping line. Finally I called the president of the line.

I introduced myself and found that he knew my husband. Edmund had shipped tobacco on U.S. Lines for years. The president had read in *Reader's Digest* the circumstances of

Edmund's recent death and the miracle that God had brought me down safely to tell about it.

"Are you a believer, a Christian?" I asked him.

He responded, "Yes."

"Then will you pray with me? God knows where that shipment is even if we don't. He knows it belongs to me, and He can bring it to us if we ask in faith that He hears and cares. Will you agree?" So we asked in Jesus' name.

The president of the company was the highest authority I could appeal to here on Earth, so that was all we could do. The rest was up to God.

In May, I was visiting some friends in Savannah, Georgia. There, in a dining room overlooking the Savannah River, we watched the pleasure boats, yachts and even ocean liners slip past us far below. They told me Savannah, although far inland, is a deep-sea port. Suddenly around the curve of the river a container ship appeared. Although I had never seen one before, it was unmistakable. On the broad deck were stacked the orange, blue, purple and yellow containers I had seen in the shipyards of Los Angeles and Baltimore.

"See that container ship coming around the bend?" I interjected. "I've got boxes of furniture lost on a ship like that. It's been wandering the world since August of last year. Will you pray with me that the Lord will bring it to me? He knows where it is, you know." We prayed in agreement with God's Word and with one another, then we thanked Him for the wonderful lunch, and my friends put me on the plane for Rocky Mount.

Two days later the telephone rang and Beverly's voice spoke excitedly, "Mrs. Gravely, I think we've found your furniture!"

"Where?" I asked.

"In Savannah," she replied.

"Savannah? Why I was just there last week! When did they find it?"

"Last week!" she almost shrieked.

Then she unfolded this tale: a man from the shipping office in Savannah, Georgia, called the Norfolk office to report,

The Power of Persistence in Prayer

"Beverly, I think we have found what you are looking for. We don't know for sure because there's no proper identification, but on the boxes we found one word: 'Janice.' "

"That's it!" Beverly exclaimed. "Send them on!"

When the boxes arrived at the Norfolk customs office, the customs officials compared my insurance manifest with the contents and agreed that this was indeed my shipment. They calculated the duty, and the U.S. Lines sent the boxes to me by freight, at their expense, as a courtesy for all the delay.

Two days later, when the Estes truck rolled up to my side door, the driver said, "I've been delivering shipments for twenty years, but this is the first time I have ever released one without a name or address!"

Sure enough, there were three large, wooden packing boxes with only the word 'Janice' on them.

I can only guess what happened. Possibly Patrick Tan completed my order, filled the chests with the treasures, boxed them up in three crates and labeled them "Janice," intending to finish the labeling later. Perhaps he then pushed the boxes aside until he got enough done to fill a container, then called the shipping company for a pickup. Evidently my boxes were sent off to the United States without the address having been completed. When the shipment arrived in Oakland, the Norfolk office was notified and they called me. But the dock workers that unloaded the container found three boxes with no identification other than "Janice" and put them aside. Later, the boxes were put on a freighter going through the Panama Canal to the East Coast.

That is all supposition, but only God could guide those boxes from China to my home without an address. And I'm equally certain that without prayer, they would still be lost.

In the story in Luke about the widow who pestered that judge for her case, the judge said, *"Yet because this widow keeps bothering me, I will see that she gets justice, so that she won't eventually wear me out with her coming!"* (Luke 18:5). Sounds a little like me, doesn't it? Yet God honors persistence in prayer, more than that judge.

Jesus explained further: *"And will not God bring about jus-*

tice for his chosen ones, who cry out to him day and night? Will he keep putting them off? I tell you, he will see that they get justice, and quickly. However, when the Son of Man comes, will he find faith on the earth?" (Luke 18:7-8).

The writer of the Hebrews declared: *"Without faith it is impossible to please God, because anyone who comes to him must believe that he exists, and that he rewards those who earnestly seek him"* (Hebrews 11:6).

Sometimes I have stopped just one prayer short of getting the answer I needed. Was it that last prayer in the restaurant that connected the dock worker with my boxes? When we get to Heaven we'll know. In the meantime I'm determined not to stop one prayer short of the prize because Jesus tells us that God brings justice to the chosen ones who cry out to Him day and night. God rewards persistence in prayer.

Chapter 18

Healing Comes

Healing comes. Watch for it. One of the wonders of the human body is its capacity to mend itself if rest, proper nutrition and exercise are applied with tender loving care. God made us this way.

Our bodies are the physical containers of our God-given spirit. They are *"fearfully and wonderfully made"* by God (Psalm 139:14). Therefore we have a serious obligation to care for them, well or sick. Paul wrote: *"Do you not know that your body is a temple of the Holy Spirit, who is in you, whom you have received from God? You are not your own; you were bought at a price. Therefore honor God with your body"* (1 Corinthians 6:19-20).

I was shocked to read Proverbs 18:9 in the Amplified Version. It says: *"... he who does not use his endeavors to heal himself is brother to him who commits suicide."* That warning inspires me to use every means possible to take care of my body.

When our nine-year-old daughter, Louise, was diagnosed with acute lymphatic leukemia four days before Christmas, the doctors started chemotherapy immediately, hoping to induce remission and prolong her life a year or two. Without treatment, they said, she would die within days.

We used every approach to healing available, beginning with prayer. God had put me through school on the principle of praying with dogged faith already.

Prayer

My friend Margaret and I prayed, standing on the sidewalk, as I have said, before Edmund and I left for Duke Hospital. She enlisted others to pray. The prayer support was so notable that years later, when I wrote the book *Won't Somebody Help Me!*, I was able to thank people for their part in Louise's healing.

Praise

Louise and I took our ukulele and song book with us so we could sing and praise the Lord in the hospital. Can you picture it: Louise, wan and weak, in this strange sing-along and me hunched around the tiny instrument? The two of us sang everything from *Jesus Loves the Little Children* to *Onward, Christian Soldiers*.

Certainly the singing kept up her spirits between visits by the nurses, tests and needle pricks. Definitely it gave me something to do instead of worrying. Actually we were doing battle toe-to-toe with Satan — raising up God's greatest weapon: praise. Rehearsing the great love and mighty power of Jesus built up our faith in God, leaving no room for fear to occupy our minds, emotions or spirits.

Singing praises is all God told Jehoshaphat to do when he faced the invading enemy hordes: *"When the men of Judah came to the place that overlooks the desert and looked toward the vast army, they saw only dead bodies lying on the ground; no one had escaped"* (2 Chronicles 20:21-24).[1]

Trust

We turned everything over to the Lord. Edmund was so crushed by the threat to his younger daughter's life that he turned to the Lord and met Jesus both as Savior and Burden-bearer.

Nutrition

We changed our diet. When we returned home from the hospital after the crisis of chemotherapy was past, the ravenous appetite that accompanies cortisone therapy overtook

Healing Comes

Louise. We turned to Adele Davis's *Let's Get Well*[2] for proper nutrition — always with prayer.

Guarding the Eyes and Ears

Louise's recuperation was slow. It was two months before she could go out of the house. We watched little or no television except for President Nixon's visit to China. Instead we focused on *"whatever things are true ... noble ... just ... pure ... lovely ... of good report ... virtuous and ... praiseworthy"* as Paul recommends in Philippians 4:8 (NKJ).[3] We all needed to *"be transformed by the renewing of [our] minds,"*[4] otherwise fear of the deadly blood disease would overtake us.

The Importance of the Blood

My Bible reading impressed on me the importance of the blood — the blood sacrifice for sin in the Old Testament,[5] Jesus' blood shed for our sins and the blood covenant established at the Last Supper.[6] As soon as Louise could leave the house, we began receiving communion every Wednesday and Sunday from the same caring rector who had come to Louise's bedside to anoint her with oil in the name of the Lord.[7] The concept of Christ's blood shed and His body broken for me, for Louise and for the world became vivid and powerful in my mind.

Exercise

Gradually, as Louise grew stronger, we began taking walks, then bicycle rides. Sometimes I stretched her too far, but always we acted on the belief that she was getting well.

Avoiding Negative Talk

Edmund, from the beginning, had decided that Louise didn't need to know the seriousness of her illness. This was to allay fear. We knew that fear is the opposite of faith and tends to replace it. Fear is faith in the devil and what he can do to hurt you. Faith is belief in God's ability to help you.

By spring Louise began half-days at school. Edmund went to her teachers with strict instructions that no one mention leukemia at all. Louise did not hear the word at home, and she was not to hear it at school. She had a blood disease. That's all.

The same children who had pulled her long, fat braids now taunted her as "Bald Eagle" because of the few wisps that let the shiny scalp glint through — hair loss as a result of "chemo" — but no one said the "L" word.

Praying for Others

In the fall Louise returned to school full-time, with monthly appointments at Duke because of the chemotherapy. We saw such pain and hopelessness in the other patients that we tried to share the strength we drew from Psalms 91 and 103. We found that it was very hard for people to have faith in God or His Bible if they didn't know Him already. We prayed anyhow. The Bible says *"pray for each other so that you may be healed"* (James 5:16).

Refusing to Receive A False Alarm

With almost every healing comes a temptation. The symptoms come back, and we are tempted to believe that the illness has returned. A relapse? No. It is an attempt by the Deceiver to fool us into thinking that God hasn't healed us after all — an attempt to steal what God has given. We choose whom we believe!

One night all the original symptoms came back on Louise — bleeding under the skin from any little bump, weakness and hemorrhaging from the nose. The doctor said, "Come, prepared to stay." Convinced of her healing, we took the ukulele but no nightie. To the doctors' surprise, they found no cancer cells in the bone marrow test. This was not a loss of remission. It was the collapse of her system from the che-

Healing Comes

motherapy. We returned home, back on cortisone and a lower "chemo" dosage, which was never again increased.

Years later Louise learned the name and nature of her disease. A newcomer in her Sunday school class heard that Louise had been fatally ill. She asked Louise about "her leukemia," but because she had been walking in faith three and a half years, Louise was able to resist the fear. After four years of treatment, the Lord provided a way for her to stop the "chemo" altogether. God healed Louise.

Looking back, I see that we applied some good lessons that could be helpful to others:

1. From the beginning we laid a prayer foundation, choosing faith over fear.[8]
2. We used every means at hand for healing: corporate prayer, doctors, medical treatment, good nutrition, healthy thinking and laughter, anointing with oil in the name of the Lord (see James 5:14), frequent and regular communion, exercise, renewing the mind (see Romans 12:1-2) and sharing our faith.[9]
3. Believing God for His highest and best brought many unexpected benefits, like Edmund's salvation and the experience confirmed that God was working all things together for good.[10]

Briefly, here are some actions anyone can take when healing is needed:

1. Begin with prayer and praise, continue in prayer and praise and end with prayer and praise.
2. It's hard to pray for ourselves when we are sick, so get help. Enlist others in the Body of Christ to pray with you. We do need to pray for ourselves, however, although we may not feel like it.
3. Base prayer on the promises of God. At first one may not have much faith for healing, but faith comes. Faith comes by hearing the Word of God.[11] Faith in the perfect love of God comes to replace fear and trepida-

tion. Faith comes when we choose to believe God's promises to us.

God's Promises

Healing was one of the promises of God to the children of Israel when He brought them out of Egypt. God said to the Israelites at Marah: *"If you listen carefully to the voice of the Lord your God and do what is right in his eyes, if you pay attention to his commands and keep all his decrees, I will not bring on you any of the diseases I brought on the Egyptians, FOR I AM THE LORD WHO HEALS YOU"* (Exodus 15:26) and *"The Lord will keep you free from every disease. He will not inflict on you any of the horrible diseases you knew in Egypt"* (Deuteronomy 7:15).

Healing, Part of the Atonement

The sweeping provisions of the atonement cover everything: mental and emotional illnesses, as well as ailments brought on by sin. Everything! Jesus paid for it all when He was scourged and nailed to the cross. *"Surely he took up our infirmities and carried our sorrows, yet we considered him stricken by God, smitten by him, and afflicted. But he was pierced for our transgressions, he was crushed for our iniquities; the punishment that brought our peace was upon him, and by his wounds we are healed"* (Isaiah 53:4-6).

Seven hundred years before the actual crucifixion, Isaiah prophesied that we are healed by the scourging of Jesus. Peter looked back on the atonement, putting it in the past tense: *"By his wounds you have been healed"* (1 Peter 2:24). The atonement is enough for the sins and sicknesses of the whole world. It is surely enough for my illness and yours.

The Consequences of Sin

Sin is the cause of much pain and many illnesses. One specific sin we often overlook was identified when Paul con-

Healing Comes

fronted the Corinthians with their double offense of taking communion without first examining themselves for sins. He said we must deal with sins before we come to the altar: *"Whoever eats the bread or drinks the cup of the Lord in an unworthy manner will be guilty of sinning against the body and blood of the Lord. A man ought to examine himself before he eats of the bread and drinks of the cup. For anyone who eats and drinks without recognizing the body of the Lord eats and drinks judgment on himself. That is why many among you are weak and sick, and a number of you have fallen asleep [died]. But if we judged ourselves, we would not come under judgment. When we are judged by the Lord, we are being disciplined so that we will not be condemned with the world"* (1 Corinthians 11:27-32).

Judging Our Own Sin

How do we judge ourselves to avoid this judgment? First, have a heart open to the gentle dealing of the Holy Spirit. I ask Him what's inside me that is not pleasing to Him. (If I had known, I would already have confessed it, so I need to have the Holy Spirit show me. Even David said, *"Cleanse thou me of secret faults."*[12] We all have them.) When God shows me self-pity, anger, bitterness, gossip, unforgiveness, pride or envy, then I can see it as God sees it and turn away in revulsion. I repent. I ask God to forgive me. We take refuge in the promise of God in 1 John 1:9: *"If we confess our sins, he is faithful and just to forgive us our sins and to cleanse us from all unrighteousness"* (NAS).

When we sincerely repent and confess our sins, God is faithful to forgive. He is just to cleanse us of all unrighteousness because Jesus paid the price for our sins in the atonement. We don't have to. *"It is finished."*[13]

If sickness has resulted from sin harbored in our lives, then we can expect it to yield when the sin is identified, confessed and repented of. Sickness will then yield to prayer and be lifted off because the sin base is gone. Deprived of any ground, Satan will lose his power to afflict us.

Ground Level Christianity
Mental and Emotional Illnesses

Mental and emotional illnesses are also covered in the atonement. *"The punishment that brought us peace was upon him, and by his wounds we are healed"* (Isaiah 53:5). I have found the 23rd Psalm very helpful in praying for peace.[14] When the disturbed person can cling to the words *"He restores my soul,"* they act as an anchor in the storm. *"For the word of God is living and powerful"* (Hebrews 4:12, KJV).

Anointing the Sick with Oil

Elders in the church are authorized to pray for the sick and anoint them with oil in the name of the Lord, and they will recover (see James 5:14). This promise helped me dramatically once when I was first feeling my way in the walk of faith. I went to my minister for this prayer and anointing. I had a very severe, tenacious case of cystitis which did not yield even to treatments by a specialist. When the minister asked me if I had taken the medical route, I assured him that I had used every home remedy and every professional therapy available. The only recourse left to me was to go to the elders.

This was new territory for both of us. We had no oil, so we just went into the sanctuary to kneel at the altar. There he prayed a simple prayer. It didn't seem as earth shaking or impressive as my acute suffering merited, but I thanked him and reported to my doctor. His examination showed a total healing of cystitis.

In a halting and inadequate way, I told my doctor what had happened. I wish I had known the scriptures where Samuel says *"to obey is better than sacrifice"* (1 Samuel 15:22) and where Jeremiah says that God hastens to perform His word (see Jeremiah 1:12) because all we did was obey what God said to do, and God did what He said He would do. But the doctor got the message and lost a patient. All God asks of us is to obey the truth that we know. He does the work.

Healing Comes
The Danger of Ignorance and Apathy

Often healing comes even though sin remains, but eventually sin must be dealt with. Perhaps unconfessed sin is the reason underlying the "loss of healing" that some people speak of.

Sometimes a believer, through ignorance or apathy, does not fend off the attacks of the enemy; then Satan can harass him unmercifully. Peter and James teach us to *"resist the devil"* (James 4:7 and 1 Peter 5:9).

Self-inflicted Diseases

A doctor friend, whom I'll call Dr. Lewis, observed one day; "Disease can be a complicated business and takes multiple cures, including medicines. Many of the diseases I see are self-inflicted — from dietary mismanagement, smoking, fast cars, drugs, etc." Ouch!

A Faithless Prayer

The escape hatch that undermines faith for healing is the phrase *"if it be Thy will"* which we hear tacked onto many prayers for healing. It is as if we want to let God off the hook in case the healing doesn't come when we think it should.

Jesus emphatically said it IS His will to heal. He took the stripes by which we were healed. The price is paid. He is the doctor. In Mark 1, when a man with leprosy came to Jesus, begging Him on his knees, *"If you are willing, you can make me clean"* (Mark 1:40), Jesus' response was positive: *"Filled with compassion, Jesus reached out his hand and touched the man. 'I am willing,' he said. 'Be clean!' Immediately the leprosy left him and he was cured"* (Mark 1:41-42). The King James Version puts it even more plainly: the leper says, *"If thou wilt,"* and Jesus replies, *"I will; be thou clean."* It is the will of God to heal. We can pray with that assurance because the Lord said, *"I am watching to see that my word is fulfilled"* (Jeremiah 1:12).

Ground Level Christianity
Entreating God

But we bow to God's sovereignty, knowing that He is working all things together for our good. Our good affects many people, maybe generations. Maybe nations. Consider Hezekiah's story.

Hezekiah was one of the best of the good kings of Judah. After he had proven his faith in God in a long, fruitful life, he became ill and was at the point of death. He summoned the prophet Isaiah who told him from God that he would die. In his bed Hezekiah turned his face to the wall and prayed to the Lord: " *'Remember, O LORD, how I have walked before you faithfully and with wholehearted devotion and have done what is good in your eyes.' And Hezekiah wept bitterly. Then the word of the LORD came to Isaiah: 'Go tell Hezekiah, "This is what the LORD, the God of your father David, says: I have heard your prayer and seen your tears; I will add fifteen years to your life" ' "* (Isaiah 38:3-5, see also 2 Kings 20:1-11).

During those next fifteen years Hezekiah sired a son, Manasseh, who succeeded to the throne when he was only twelve years old. He was the most wicked king Judah ever had. The nation lost its godly heritage, fell into idolatry and was defeated and deported by Nebuchadnezzar to Babylon. The moral of this story is: God knows best. He can be entreated by prayer, but He gives the best to those who leave the choice to Him.

Death Comes

Sometimes, despite the prayers of faith, persistence and perseverance on the part of the sick person, death comes prematurely. This was the case in our family. In the midst of all this faith and victory, Peyton died. At the age of thirty-seven, he and Kim were the parents of four young children and had their whole lives ahead of them. Doctors, however, told him he had scleroderma and could expect only five to eight more years to live. Scleroderma is sometimes referred to as "the turning-to-stone disease" because all the soft tis-

Healing Comes

sue in the body becomes hard, causing the organs to lose their function. Only a miracle could avert an early death.

Peyton loved Jesus and the Word of God. He knew how to believe God's Word over any circumstances, how to exercise faith, how to stand in the strength and power of God, and having done all, to stand. His family, also strong in the faith, stood too, believing God for healing until the end. For seven years he got closer and closer to God — until one day he went to Heaven.

More than once during that time Peyton asked, "Where's my miracle? Louise had hers; Mom had hers; where's mine?" We don't know the answer to that question. An old hymn says:

> *Farther along we'll know all about it.*
> *Farther along we'll understand why.*

In the meantime we look to God, knowing that He is a good God who gives good gifts to His children.

One day Isaiah 57:1-2 came alive for me when I read: *"The good men perish; the godly die before their time .... No one seems to realize that God is taking them away from evil days ahead. For the godly who die shall rest in peace"* (TLB).

The Best Medicine: A Happy Heart

The best medicine, of course, is a joyful heart: *"A happy heart is good medicine and a cheerful mind works healing, but a broken spirit dries up the bones"* (Proverbs 17:22, AMP). So much healing is needed for those with a broken spirit. They want to have a happy heart and a cheerful mind, but their illness prevents it. Or does it? Jesus took this, too, in the Great Exchange, the atonement. Jesus read the first part of this Isaiah passage in the synagogue when He announced His commission to the Jews: *"The Spirit of the Sovereign LORD is on me, because the LORD has anointed me to preach good news to the poor. He has sent me to bind up the brokenhearted, to proclaim freedom for the captives and release from darkness for the prison-*

ers, to proclaim the year of the LORD's favor and the day of vengeance of our God, to comfort all that mourn, and provide for those who grieve in Zion — to bestow in them a crown of beauty instead of ashes, the oil of gladness instead of mourning, and a garment of praise instead of a spirit of despair" (Isaiah 61:1-3).

It's hard for the broken-spirited to climb up the ladder out of the hole they're in. With some help, though, they can exercise their faith, pray, ask others to pray and believe the Word of God for the crown of beauty, the oil of gladness and the garment of praise to replace their despair.

When one part of a person is ill, because body, mind and spirit are all related, sometimes it affects the other parts. That is why the atonement had to cover it all.

An Action Alert!

Even though I know that Jesus has already paid the price for my healing, illness alerts me to do everything possible to get well: spiritually, mentally and physically, not neglecting any part.

Recently I had a complete physical examination from Dr. Lewis. I was chilly and miserable inside the crackling disposable paper apron and vest, but the results of the exam were heartwarming.

Two years before this appointment, my chiropractor said, "Janice, there's nothing I can do for you. You need to see a medical doctor." The pain in my back had been identified as osteoporosis and finally, after a year, I went to Dr. Lewis, who helped me. Meanwhile I took everything in the medicine cabinet for relief. I couldn't sleep very well. In the morning it took me two hours to loosen up. After that, the agony subsided to pain or dull ache, although walking helped. Was there a connection between this back pain and an emotional pain I had suffered in the recent past? Yes, I thought so.

Later, dressed and warm, I sat in Dr. Lewis' office, waiting for his report. He seemed unhurried as he began, "Everything checks out well here, Janice. I'll send you a com-

Healing Comes

plete report of the lab work in the mail. The best thing to do with it is to put the report into your suitcase so it will be with you when you're away from home. In case you need medical attention, it will tell the doctor there what he needs to know about your case. You don't have either allergies or special medication — except Estrogen. The report looks official, but it's nothing to worry about. Your checkup went very well."

If he could ramble, maybe I could, too. "Dr. Lewis, experience leads me to believe that I don't get sick without a reason. I believe that when God saved me He redeemed my body as well as my soul. I'm His child, and this body belongs to Him, too. He made provision for healing my spirit, soul and body in the atonement which covers everything. He keeps me well — unless I hinder Him by sin or unforgiveness or, in this case, by hurt feelings. About two years ago I had a head-on collision with an authority figure, and I suffered a severe emotional hurt.

"For me, hurt feelings pinpoint a vulnerable place — some dirt in me that the Lord wants to clean up. Later, I was wounded again — so hurt it 'made me sick at my stomach,' as we say. It was a one-two punch to my body's natural defense system. Since I hadn't dealt with the previous hurt, God's healing provisions weren't working for me.

"That was when my back gave way — a natural result of my age, heredity, ten years of no exercise — and hurt feelings. Osteoporosis. Natural, yes, but not anything God put on me. Like the proverb says, *"A broken spirit dries up the bones."*[15]

"So, when I forgave the offenses as completely as God does mine — and He separated my sin of hurt and self-pity as far from me as the east is from the west[16] — and when that spirit of manipulation and control was gone (it took a while for him to get me delivered of that) — then the block to God's healing provision was gone, too. The healing came."

Dr. Lewis heard me out and seemed to agree that my spiritual illness was connected with the physical illness. So I asked

Ground Level Christianity

the Big Question. "Would you say that my back is healed, then? No osteoporosis?"

"Yes, Janice," he replied, "I'd say your back is healed."

Yes, healing comes, and when it doesn't, we must trust God.

The writer to the Hebrews said in his famous chapter on faith (Hebrews 11) that it is impossible to please God without faith. He noted that some men and women received their faith-filled requests, while others died without relief to their sufferings. The writer drew this conclusion: *"Let us run with perseverance the race marked out for us"* (Hebrews 12:1).

Meanwhile, God is working all things together for our good. Most people I know who have been through an ordeal waiting for healing say that much good has come out of it. While our body or soul is healing, we usually draw closer to God in our need. We can see close-up the hand of the Redeemer at work in our lives as the healing comes.

Endnotes: Healing Comes

1. **2 Chronicles 20:20-24**—Early in the morning they left for the Desert of Tekoa. As they set out, Jehoshaphat stood and said, "Listen to me, Judah and people of Jerusalem! Have faith in the LORD your God and you will be upheld; have faith in his prophets and you will be successful." After consulting the people, Jehoshaphat appointed men to sing to the LORD, and to praise him for the splendor of his holiness as they went out at the head of the army, saying:
"Give thanks to the LORD for his love endures forever."
As they began to sing and praise, the LORD set ambushes against the men of Ammon and Moab and Mount Seir who were invading Judah, and they were defeated. The men of Ammon and Moab rose up against the men from Mount Seir to destroy and annihilate them. After they finished slaughtering the men from Seir, they helped to destroy one another.
When the men of Judah came to the place that overlooks the desert and looked toward the vast army, they saw only dead bodies, lying on the ground; no one had escaped.

Healing Comes

2. Davis, Adele, *Let's Get Well* (New York, Harcourt Brace Jovanovich, Inc., 1970)
3. **Philippians 4:8**—Finally, brothers, whatever is true, whatever is noble, whatever is right, whatever is pure, whatever is lovely, whatever is admirable — if anything is excellent or praiseworthy — think about such things.
4. **Romans 12:1-2**—Therefore, I urge you, brothers, in view of God's mercy, to offer your bodies as living sacrifices, holy and pleasing to God — which is your spiritual act of worship. Do not conform any longer to the pattern of this world, but be transformed by the renewing of your mind.
5. The first blood sacrifice recorded was by Abel, who brought portions from the firstborn of his flock, which pleased the Lord (see Genesis 4:4). God Himself cut a blood covenant with Abram (see Genesis 15:9-20) and ordained blood sacrifice for sin (see Leviticus 4-9 and 23, Hebrews 9:12-14 and John 19:34).
   Hebrews 9:22—In fact, the law requires that nearly everything be cleansed with blood, and without the shedding of blood there is no forgiveness.
6. **Matthew 26:26**—While they were eating, Jesus took bread, gave thanks and broke it, and gave it to his disciples, saying, "Take and eat; this is my body." Then he took the cup, gave thanks and offered it to them, saying, "Drink from it, all of you. This is my blood of the covenant, which is poured out for many for the forgiveness of sins.
7. **James 5:14-15**—Is any one of you sick? He should call the elders of the church to pray over him and anoint him with oil in the name of the Lord. And the prayer offered in faith will make the sick person well; the Lord will raise him up.
8. **1 John 4:18**—Perfect love casts out fear (NAS).
9. **James 5:16**—Therefore confess your sins to each other and pray for each other so that you may be healed. The prayer of a righteous man in powerful and effective.
10. **Romans 8:28**—And we know that in all things God works for the good of those who love him, who have been called according to his purpose.
11. **Romans 10:17**—So then faith comes by hearing, and hearing by the word of God (NKJ).

12. **Psalm 19:12**—Who can discern his errors? Forgive my hidden faults.
13. **John 19:30**—When he had received the drink, Jesus said, "It is finished." With that, he bowed his head and gave up his spirit.
14. **Psalm 23:4**—Even though I walk through the valley of the shadow of death, I will fear no evil, for you are with me; your rod and your staff, they comfort me.
15. **Proverbs 17:22**—A cheerful heart is good medicine, but a crushed spirit dries up the bones.
16. **Psalm 103:12**—As far as the east is from the west, so far has he removed our transgressions from us.

Chapter 19

"What Must I Do to Be Saved?"[1]

"Sirs, what must I do to be saved?" cried the Philippian jailer to Paul and Silas when God miraculously opened the prison to free His servants. The jailer fell on his knees before them and begged them for his life. *"Believe in the Lord Jesus, and you will be saved,"* Paul replied. *"Then they [Paul and Silas] spoke the word of the Lord to him and all the others in his house"* (Acts 16:30-34).

What is *"the Word of the Lord"* that can save all who hear it? It is the Gospel. It is like light to men's souls. When the truth of the Gospel comes in, the darkness cannot put it out. The truth is that Jesus came into the world to save sinners (see 1 Timothy 1:15). The truth is *"... that Christ died for our sins according to the Scriptures, that he was buried, that he was raised on the third day according to the Scriptures"* (1 Corinthians 15:3-4). This is the Gospel in a nutshell.

Perhaps the form most familiar to denominational Christians is found in the Apostles' Creed or the Nicene Creed. The Apostles' Creed says: "I believe in God, the Father Almighty, Maker of heaven and earth, and in Jesus Christ, his only Son, our Lord; who was conceived by the Virgin Mary, suffered under Pontius Pilate, was crucified, dead and buried; (he descended into Hell), he arose on the third day and sits on the right hand of God the Father; from thence he shall come to judge the quick and the dead. I believe in the Holy Spirit, the holy catholic church, the forgiveness of sins and the life everlasting."

However we express it, the Gospel is powerful. Paul said, *"I am not ashamed of the gospel, because it is the power of God for the salvation of everyone who believes"* (Romans 1:16). The power is in the truth and in believing the truth. Jesus turned the disciples loose with this truth, and they turned the world upside down.[2]

Jesus charged His followers: *"go and make disciples of all nations ... . And surely I am with you always, to the very end of the age"* (Matthew 28:19-20). But first He said: *"All authority in heaven and on earth has been given to me. Therefore [in my name] go ... ."* Not only did Jesus have all authority but He gave it to his followers when He told them (and us) to use His Name.

Jesus also promised that supernatural signs would accompany those who believe and preach the Gospel: *"In my name they will drive out demons; they will speak in new tongues; ... they will place their hands on sick people, and they will get well ... . Then the disciples went out and preached everywhere, and the Lord worked with them and confirmed his word by the signs that accompanied it"* (Mark 16:17-18 and 20).

"Make Disciples"

Sometimes God wants you and me to share the Gospel with a person He has prepared. What should we do then? We can take a lesson from the book of Revelation which says, *"They overcame him [the Adversary] with the blood of the Lamb and by the word of their testimony"* (Revelation 12:11). In other words, tell the person your testimony — how you got saved.

Then, if you haven't fainted from fright and the person hasn't fled, you can mention Jesus and His conversation with Nicodemus when He said, *"No one can see the kingdom of God unless he is born again"* (John 3:3) and *"You must be born again"* (John 3:7). Ask if the person you are talking to wants to be in the Kingdom of Heaven. Most people answer yes.

Now, it's wise to be sensitive to the leading of the Holy Spirit. As the scripture says, *"I [Paul] planted the seed, Apollos watered it, but God made it grow"* (1 Corinthians 3:6). Maybe today you are planting, and someone else will harvest later. However, if the person has not turned you off, and if you feel to continue, a good next step is the "Two Questions" of Evangelism Explosion.[3]

"What Must I Do To Be Saved?"

First ask: "If you were to die tonight, where would you spend eternity?" Most people will respond with hope that it will be in Heaven.

Then ask: "If you were to die tonight and stood before God, and He asked you, 'Why should I let you into My Heaven?' what would you say?"

The answer pretty well tells you what this person is depending on for his or her salvation. Is it a belief that he or she is a "good person," or belief in Jesus' sacrificial death on the cross to atone for our sins? If the person is unsure of what to say, roll out the power of the Gospel, because it is *"the power of God unto salvation."*

It helps to say "I believe ..." and quote the Apostles' Creed. Church members of many denominations know the creed by heart without realizing that it is the Gospel. It is a widely accepted statement of Christian faith.

If your friend knows the truth of the Gospel and believes that God raised Jesus from the dead in the mighty resurrection,[4] then you can go on. However, not all churchgoers are firm on that point, so the Bible is the best tool for the task. All four of the gospels give accounts of the resurrection. It is one of the most well-documented events in history, so it is not really open to question. Either the person believes history and the Bible or refuses. If the individual does not believe the Bible, it may be time to ease off because this person may not be ready to accept the truth.

If, on the other hand, the person seems willing to continue, with these obstacles behind you, he [or she] is ready to seal the commitment. Show him Romans 10:8-10 and 13. It says: *"The word [of faith] is near you; it is in your mouth and in your heart .... If you confess with your mouth, 'Jesus is [my] Lord,' and believe in your heart that God raised Him from the dead, you will be saved. For it is with your heart that you believe and are justified, and it is with your mouth that you confess and are saved .... For 'Everyone who calls on the name of the Lord will be saved.'"*

The eternal matter being settled here is the Lordship of

Ground Level Christianity

Jesus Christ in the life of the believer. With this confession of faith in Jesus, your friend has unseated Self and Satan from the throne of his life and given that place to Jesus. He has been *"delivered ... from the power of darkness, and ... translated ... into the Kingdom of his [God's] dear Son"*[5] by faith in the blood shed for him by Jesus on the cross.

Now what would your friend say to God when asked "Why should I let you into My Heaven?" He could say "I have faith in Jesus' work, not my own."[6] (He might need a little coaching on this point.) Now what would your friend say when asked where he will spend eternity? He can resoundingly say, "In Heaven, with my Lord Jesus!" — or words to that effect.

Finally, seal the commitment with a prayer. Up to now the person hasn't confessed sins and asked forgiveness. With his newly awakened sensitivity to sin, he will be glad to know how to recognize his sin and repent of it. Your prayer will show him the way.

Confession of Sins

Of course, every case is different.

There was Dreama, who was so thrilled to be a Christian that she confessed and shed forty-three years of misery, hatred and sin when she learned the power of 1 John 1:9: *"If we confess our sins, he is faithful and just and will forgive us our sins and purify us from all unrighteousness."* Only when the Holy Spirit, whose job it is to convict of sin, had entered and given Dreama's spirit new life, did she perceive that there were sins in her life. Only when she knew that God forgives sin because of what Jesus has done on her behalf could she confess, receive forgiveness and be FREE.

Like a Marriage Vow

Then there was Penny. Penny was a grandmother whose red hair and beauty had given her the name. We were en-

"What Must I Do To Be Saved?"

joying steamy, fragrant coffee at her daughter's kitchen table when Penny said, "I've gone to church until I'm sick of it. There is nothing there for me. Same old songs, same old sermon, same old smiles on the faces of the people who don't know what trouble is. I pray, but nothing happens. God doesn't notice. My life is so hard right now that I'm desperate."

"Jesus notices. He can help you," I put in gently. "Do you know Jesus? He knows you."

"How can you know Jesus?" she challenged.

"Well, the Bible says that He is the Lover of your soul; that your Maker is your husband, and that no weapon formed against you can prosper, and every tongue that rises up against you, you will refute (see Isaiah 54:5 and 17). Would you like to have Jesus for your Lord, your Master, your Husband?"

"Well, yes — I sure do need something."

"Well, it's kind of like a marriage, Penny. If you take Him, He takes you. Would you like that?" When she nodded, I pressed on. "Penny, repeat after me: I, Penny..."

"I, Penny..."

"Take thee, Jesus..."

"Take thee, Jesus..."

"To be my Lord and Savior..."

"To be my Lord and Savior..."

"To have and to hold from this day forward into eternity." She repeated it, and we went on to say, "I believe that You are the Son of God, and that You died for my sins on the cross and shed Your blood to ransom me out of the hand of Satan. I believe that God raised You from the dead, You are living in Heaven, and You have made a place for me to be with You forever. Thank You, Jesus, for coming into my heart and saving me. I will live for You and try to please You. Forgive me of my sins and set me on the path to walk with You. In Jesus' Name I pray."

Our tears salted the coffee cups as Jesus made Himself real to Penny as her Lord, Savior and Husband.

Ground Level Christianity
Testifying to Children

Children are very easy to bring into the Kingdom of God. Usually they know stories about Jesus, which are comforting and reassuring. When you ask them if they want Jesus to come into their hearts, to be their Lord and Savior, it seems like a logical and agreeable proposal to them. Just the simplest statement about Jesus being the Son of God and God raising Him from the dead is often enough. If the children have had any church background at all, they believe that Jesus is God's Son and accept the resurrection as fact, having been told about it by people they trust. A prayer which they say out loud will seal the covenant.

My daughter, Louise, was about four and a half years old when she was born again. She was sick, lying on the sofa and feeling worse than bad. She looked so miserable I was prompted to ask, "Louise, is something bothering you? I mean something besides not feeling well?"

She gave me a noncommittal "Mmmm," so I went on.

"What do you do with the bad feelings that come when you don't tell the truth? When you are mean to Ginger? When you disobey?"

She looked at me, seeming almost thankful that somebody knew that there were bad feelings inside her.

"Would you like to get those bad feelings out?" I asked gently, "They come from sin, you know, and sin can make you feel worse and worse, unless you let Jesus help you. Jesus died for your sins, and He can take them away. Do you want Jesus to be your Savior and Lord?"

"Oh, yes," she said with great relief and expectation.

With a little help, she prayed a prayer, asking Jesus to be her Savior and Lord and to forgive her sins. When she lifted her head, there was the life of Christ shining in her eyes.

When Jesus comes into a life there usually is an immediate, discernible change in that person's eyes. *"The true light that gives light to every man"* (John 1:9) shines out of the newborn spirit where light has replaced darkness. As you are

"What Must I Do To Be Saved?"

ministering to that person, look directly into his eyes from time to time to see what's in there. Your gift of the discerning of spirits[7] tells you what spirit is there. When you see the light come on, you know that Jesus has entered that spirit, and you may share that with your friend. It's very reassuring.

These few examples of the power of the Gospel show that extending God's Kingdom is as natural as breathing, when you know that it does not depend on you but on God. He wants the job done[8] and will use anyone who is willing and obedient to do the work.

Christ's Great Commission[9] to preach the Gospel is given to all of His followers. Jesus promised to work with us confirming the Word with signs that follow. The responsibility rests with the Holy Spirit to use our obedience as He chooses.

Whenever God uses us to help bring someone into His Kingdom, we have further responsibility to that soul. Follow-up is very necessary. In the family, following up is manageable. In Sunday school, let the parents know of the child's decision and help them to understand what has happened and what comes next. Be sensitive in this area. Often the Lord will use the conversion of a child to bring other family members to salvation, too.

What if this encounter ends when you get off the airplane and you never see the person again for follow-up? Pray. Pray that he will find fellowship with like-minded believers, that he will build up his *"most holy faith"* as Jude says,[10] with Bible study, prayer, worship and fellowship, the four activities fundamental to Christian growth.

Leave something in his hand. I usually carry a pocket-size Bible with me and say, "Let's see what the Bible says. I think I've got one here..." as I fish it from my pocketbook, sometimes with a tract explaining the new birth. With a pencil, I underline the passages in John 3, Romans 10, Colossians 1:13 and 2 Corinthians 5:17, turning down the pages so he can find them again easily. Then I give it to him. If there is no Bible to give away, write these references on a piece of paper for him.

Ground Level Christianity

Maybe the person is ill or in trouble. While faith is high, you may need to lay hands on him and pray for him in the name of Jesus. Explain that Scripture teaches that Christ has given us authority to pray for the sick (see Mark 16:18 and James 5:14-16).

Declare That There Is No Exit

In every case, encourage the person to tell others of his salvation. The great soul-winner Billy Graham says that we need to tell someone of our new commitment. Why? So it will be set in stone. When we, by our creative word, say, "I made Jesus my Lord last night," at least three people hear it: myself, my friend and Satan. Now there is no turning back. Now Satan can't steal the joy of our salvation by saying, "Nothing really happened to you last night." The back door has been slammed shut, and there is no exit.

Is This the One?

The salvation of others doesn't depend on us. It depends on God and His purpose to extend His Kingdom until the full number have come in. He's given us the privilege of being co-workers with Him, and since He is the Great Redeemer, He can redeem anything — even a bumbling, stumbling attempt on our part to tell someone about Jesus. Remember, the power is in the Gospel, not in us. It is the truth of the Gospel that sets men free.

Not everyone will fall on his knees in front of you and beg to be saved like the Philippian jailer did with Paul and Silas, so simply ask Jesus if this is the one He has prepared for the entrance of the truth of the Gospel today. Then plunge in, expecting God to work, confirming His Word with signs that follow. And the one whom God has prepared will do what he must to be saved.

"What Must I Do To Be Saved?"

Endnotes: "What Must I Do to Be Saved?"

1. **Acts 16:30**—He then brought them out and asked, "Sirs, what must I do to be saved?
2. **Acts 17:5-6**—But the Jews ... moved with envy ... gathered a company ... crying, These that have turned the world upside down are come hither also (KJV).
3. Evangelism Explosion is a method of spreading the Gospel in a systematic way. It was developed by Dr. D. James Kennedy of Coral Ridge Ministries, in Coral Gables, Florida
4. **Luke 24:46**—He [Jesus] told them, "This is what is written: The Christ will suffer and rise from the dead on the third day ... ."
5. **Colossians 1:13**—For he has rescued us from the dominion of darkness and brought us into the kingdom of the Son he loves.
6. **Ephesians 2:8-9**—For it is by grace you have been saved, through faith—and this not from yourselves, it is the gift of God — not by works, so that no one can boast.
7. **1 Corinthians 12:10**—... to another distinguishing between spirits ...
8. **1 Timothy 1:15**—Here is a trustworthy saying that deserves full acceptance: Christ Jesus came into the world to save sinners ... .
9. **Matthew 28:18**—[The Great Commission] Then Jesus came to them and said, "All authority in heaven and on earth has been given to me. Therefore go and make disciples of all nations, baptizing them in the name of the Father and of the Son and of the Holy Spirit, and teaching them to obey everything I have commanded you. And surely I am with you always, to the very end of the age."
10. **Jude 20**—But you, dear friends, build yourselves up in your most holy faith and pray in the Holy Spirit.

Chapter 20

Humility: Who Needs It?

Recently I was bemoaning, in my prayers, some very bad decisions I had made. I said, "Dear God, if You will only sell that real estate in which I invested so unwisely, I'll never again make a decision without first finding out from You what Your will is in the situation." The truth is that sometimes I just made a decision to get on with the matter. This time I really meant it when I resolved to ask God first.

Just as gently as a loving father, He spoke to my understanding and said, "Janice, I want to lead and guide you. I am able to do this. But you do not take time to ask and find out what My will for you is. I want to help you in purchases — laser printer, Christmas shopping — and in all your decisions. I want to help you spend your time wisely. So ask Me — first, instead of afterwards."

Then the verses of Luke 11:9-10 came to mind: *"Ask and it will be given to you; seek and you will find; knock and the door will be opened to you. For everyone who asks receives; he who seeks finds; and to him who knocks, the door will be opened."*

God knew that I had wasted scores of years wondering how to humble myself under the mighty hand of God, when the answer was right there for me to ask and find out. It was not a rebuke — just the answer I needed.

Why did it take so long for me to understand what to ask and what to seek? Because, as James says, *"When you ask, you do not receive, because you ask with the wrong motives, that you may spend what you get on your pleasures"* (James 4:3).

Motives are the key — right motives. That's what God wants for us. Truth in the inward parts, as David prayed.

One way to pray with right motives is to ask God for what He has already told us He wants for us — His best. To me,

Humility: Who Needs It?

this is connected with humility, and it means talking to God about everything — FIRST.

Pride is the opposite: It says, "I can do it myself." That is shorthand for "I don't need God." No wonder that pride and self-sufficiency are abhorrent to Him.

James quotes Proverbs 3:34, saying: " *'God opposes the proud, but gives grace to the humble.' Submit yourselves, then, to God. Resist the devil, and he will flee from you. Come near to God and He will come near to you ... . Humble yourselves before the Lord, and He will lift you up"* (James 4:6-8 and 10).

Humble Myself?

We tend to think of humility as self-effacing modesty, hand-wringing hypocrisy, and an inability to take a compliment, or even fawning behavior or servile compliance. Who needs that?

In the dictionary humility is "the condition of being humble, lacking in pride." It is "marked by **meekness or** modesty in behavior, attitude or spirit; showing **deferential** or submissive respect; low in rank or unpretentious."[1] What does that mean? "Meek" is defined by the world and our dictionary as "showing patience and humility; easily imposed upon; submissive."

So why is there such a high priority put upon meekness in the Bible? In the New Testament Jesus said, *"Blessed are the meek, for they will inherit the earth"* (Matthew 5:5) and described Himself as *"meek and lowly in heart"* (Matthew 11:29, KJV).[2]

In Old Testament times Moses is described as *"very meek, above all the men which were upon the face of the earth"* (Numbers 12:3, KJV), yet Moses defied Pharaoh, led three million people out of Egypt, caused the Red Sea to part before the multitude and led them all to safety. He was the commanding general when the Israelites defeated the hostile nations in the wilderness east of the Jordan River. He led his people victoriously for forty years, all this after his eightieth birthday.

Ground Level Christianity

This is a record of strength in a *"meek"* man. It sounds desirable. It is desirable and available. We can choose to be that way. Jesus was meek, and He wants us to be meek and humble too.

Peter and James, disciples of Jesus, both tell us to *"humble [ourselves] ... under the mighty hand of God, that he may exalt [us] in due time"* (1 Peter 5:6, KJV, see also James 4:6). First, however, we are told to draw near to God, and He will draw near to us. This is what Jesus did.

Surely there is a quicker way than spending forty years in the desert, especially if you don't aspire to be a Moses. So what does a twentieth-century Christian do to become humble and meek? Seek God and wait for Him to lead or to answer, depending on the situation. The servant waits for the master, and we should wait on the Lord.

Paul said that Jesus is the head of the Body (His Church), but He does not force us to be submissive to Him. He certainly deserves our submission, but He does not require it.

This is the way we draw near to God. This is the way we humble ourselves. This is the way we partake of God's strength instead of our own weakness.

Who needs humility? Anyone who wants peace with God and the security that He brings into all the circumstances of life. Humility is part of *Ground Level Christianity*.

Endnotes: Humility: Who Needs It?

1. Humble: *The American Heritage Dictionary,* Second Edition (Boston: Houghton Mifflin Company, 1985) p. 627.
2. **Matthew 11:29**—Take my yoke upon you and learn from me, for I am gentle and humble in heart, and you will find rest for your souls.

Chapter 21

Worship

Worship is divine communication. It is a privilege only God's people can have. We come into the presence of our Heavenly Father, our Maker, with thanks and adoration and profound openness. We share with Him our innermost thoughts and seek Him, to know Him better and to hear what He has to say to us.

Mankind has always worshiped something or someone. Too often that something or someone has been a false god or myth or philosophy or money. Christian worship is different from all other worship because of Jesus who is forever alive. We worship a living God, not an idol or some figment of our imaginations. We worship a God whose love for us is great enough to sacrifice His own life in order to spare ours. We worship a God who loves us even though He knows us completely, even to our depths. We worship a God who defeated Satan and all the powers of evil on our behalf.

Because of Jesus, we can approach God *"with confidence, so that we may receive mercy and find grace to help us in time of need"* (Hebrews 4:16).

God has provided worship for us to draw near to Him with sincere hearts in full assurance of faith, cleansed from a guilty conscience and washed with the pure water of the Spirit (see Hebrews 10:22). He delights in our coming to Him.

We don't have to know all this to enter into worship of God, but it helps. We can worship God anywhere, any time because we are His children.

The Father seeks people to worship Him in Spirit and in truth, as Jesus said (see John 4:23). God is always ready to receive our worship. We can sing to Him. We can dance before Him. We can kneel, we can stand and we can lift our hands in praise, adoration and worship. We can sing in the Spirit language or sing *"with the understanding."* We can behold His marvelous creation and breathe out our thanksgiving and praise. Our Father receives it all.

Because we are members of the Body of Christ, there is a special entrance into God's presence given to us when we worship as a Body. I refer to the Church, with Jesus as the Head. We need each other to be complete. When we worship together, we are part of a whole. This is far more powerful and productive than worshiping alone.

In Psalm 100, the pattern is given like this: *"Enter his gates with thanksgiving, and his courts with praise"* (verse 4). Visualize the Tabernacle in the wilderness, and see the curtain fencing off the Holy Place of God, accessed by a gate. How grateful we are to be coming into the presence of God! One psalm says, *"I rejoiced with those who said to me, 'Let us go to the house of the LORD'"* (Psalm 122:1). We are eager and glad to go to church! God is holding court, and our entrance pass is praise.

How Can Anyone Praise God? How Can I?

I used to think that the greater always praises the lesser. The parent can praise a child, the teacher a student, the master a slave. But how can it be reversed? Then I watched David in the Psalms overflow with praise for God, for *who* He is and *what* He does, and I joined David in praise. My heart wants to praise God. My arms want to fly up into the air toward God. My body wants to bow before His Majesty. My hands want to clap and play the tambourine with the holy music, and my feet want to dance. My whole being — spirit, soul and body — wants to praise God.

When we are alone, this is possible, but when we are with others in the Body of Christ, and we are all entering into praise, it is far more wonderful. We can sense God's delight and Jesus' satisfaction. For this He died, so He could be the

Worship

firstborn of many brethren (see Romans 8:29), so God could have a people to fellowship with — *"in Spirit and in truth."*

This is the way David worshiped. No wonder he was a man after God's own heart! Some people worship quietly and others quite loudly. What is important is that it be true worship and not some form or formula.

God is worthy of our praise. Let's not give all our attention, our praise and our worship to our children, our possessions or ourselves. None of these are worthy of worship. Only Almighty God is worthy of our adoration. To worship anything less is to demean ourselves, to diminish God's creation and to debase the divine Holy Spirit within us.

The act of worship ennobles a Christian. Worship rightly relates a member of the Body of Christ with the rest of the Body and with the Head, Jesus. Worship connects us with our Maker, our Father and the Divine Architect of the Universe. We come away enriched, inspired, equipped and enabled to move in His perfect will and to accomplish His purposes in our lives and in the world. Worship is spiritual food.

Worship was the cure for a severe case of depression for Kim after the birth of her third child. This was a baby she had prayed for, and Kim knew she was a gift from God. The days following the birth were easier than with the previous two because Kim knew what to expect and how to care for the infant. Why, then, did this horrible emptiness creep over Kim before she left the hospital?

This is how Kim describes what worship did for her: "It should have been one of the most joyful times of my life. I had a wonderful marriage, we were financially secure, had just finished renovations to our home, and, best of all, our third child had just been born. And she was an angel.

"I lay in my hospital room with my tiny baby daughter, named Angelyn, in the bed beside me vigorously sucking on my little finger (our nurse didn't believe in pacifiers), and I wondered why I felt such a dragging downward in my spirit. There was no reason for such feelings. My friends and

Ground Level Christianity

family all came to see us. Peyton brought the other two children in to see their little sister, and they were adorable — patiently waiting to take turns holding the dainty little girl. And they were so careful with her. I knew they would both be a big help once we returned home.

"I also had the emotional support of a wonderful group of women friends with whom I had deep, satisfying relationships. We all gathered once a week for prayer, Bible study and fellowship. This was our real spiritual feeding time. They came to see us in the hospital, bringing gifts and laughter and happy plans for my homecoming.

"But even in the laughter I felt a hollowness, an emptiness that I couldn't explain. I had brought Andrew Murray's book on prayer to the hospital with me, along with my Bible, of course, but the joy I had always had in this kind of meditation did not come. For the first time in many years, I felt that God had turned away from me, that He did not hear my increasingly fervent prayers.

"As the days passed after we returned home, the emptiness inside me grew at a frightening rate. I felt I was being dragged downward into a black pit from which I could not escape, and the sadness I had begun to feel in the hospital became overwhelming. The presence and comfort of God in my life, on which I had come to rely daily, was gone. But I still continued to seek Him. I read my Bible and prayed continually, desperately seeking God's presence, His help, a sign ... anything. But there was only silence.

"With a trusted friend and counselor I examined myself for sin, as Paul urges in 1 Corinthians 11 and I confessed them all — even the most minute bad thought. I asked God for forgiveness because I know that unconfessed sin can be an obstacle to healing.

"The first Sunday after I came home no one expected me to go to church (the baby was only nine days old), but I had a deep need to attend the service. If God wouldn't meet with me privately, maybe I could find Him in the presence of the Body of Christ at worship.

"I tried to join in singing the opening hymn, but the tears

Worship

started to form, so I just mouthed the words in an effort to control myself.

"The following week I continued to experience profound sadness and despair. Nothing I had formerly enjoyed interested me, and I began to think of death constantly. I reached out to family members and to my friends, but no one seemed to understand. One well-meaning relative said, 'Well honey, I think you just have a little case of post-partum depression, don't you?' I shook my head, appalled at her profound lack of comprehension of the emotional pain I was suffering.

"I was still preparing meals, taking care of the children and, outwardly, continuing with my many duties as I always had. Peyton didn't see, and no one else saw, that when he and the children went off to work and to school, I paced the floor of our living room, trying to wipe away the tears, sometimes unable to stop myself from moaning aloud as I walked — crying and praying to God to save me, to rescue me from the pit.

"The following Sunday, Peyton asked if I felt like going to church again. I told him, yes, I did want to go, but to a different church — a Spirit-filled church I had visited once or twice in the past. 'Peyton,' I told him, 'I have to get some help, and I know that there isn't any for me at our church. I'm going to the Pentecostal church. Maybe the pastor will pray for me there.'

"So I went to the Pentecostal church, taking only Angelyn in my arms. This was something I would never have done under any other circumstances. I would have considered it 'breaking up our family.' But I was desperate.

"Our family would be broken apart anyway if I couldn't get well. Fear of a complete mental breakdown — of delirium, hallucinations and even suicide — had become a constant dread.

"I was greeted by an usher at the door of the church. He told me how pretty the baby was and offered to take me to the nursery. But I said I wanted to hold her. She wasn't any trouble. Actually, I needed to hold the baby. Caring for her was my strongest tie to reality. She kept me from descending deeper into my private Hell.

"I took a seat in the last pew of the sanctuary, and the service began. The music was beautiful. There were hymn books, but no one used them. Most of the words to the songs were flashed onto the wall behind the pulpit with an overhead projector. And the congregation enthusiastically sang the choruses over and over. They were meaningful songs, all giving praise to God and telling of His mercy and greatness.

"Just as the week before, I wasn't able to sing the words along with everyone else because I was weeping, but no one seemed to care if I cried.

"One woman stood up, loudly testifying of her love for God and of what He had done in her life. She was crying audibly. Many in the congregation clapped their hands. These people were in love with God, and their worship expressed that fact openly.

"Surrounded by people who were freely and unashamedly praising and worshiping the Father, I felt soothed, and the pain and darkness of my depression was eased. Here was a measure of relief — the first I had found since Angelyn's birth.

"The pastor delivered a message which began with a reading from the Bible, *'But an hour is coming, and now is, when the true worshipers shall worship the Father in spirit and truth; for such people the Father seeks to be His worshipers'* (John 4:23-24, NAS). The subject of his sermon was worship, and his purpose was to teach his flock how to draw close to God through biblical, spiritual praise.

"At the end of the service the pastor offered to pray for anyone who had needs. I responded with others, and after he had prayed for all of the others he asked several women to join him in prayer for me. That day I found some real help for my trouble.

"I found the prayers and the love and genuine concern expressed for me, a stranger, by those believers that day to

Worship

be very comforting, and what they did ministered greatly to me. Still, I was not totally rescued.

"I drove home with a measure of peace in my heart that I had not felt for several weeks, but as the hours wore on and evening approached, I knew that I was not well. As the darkness fell outside, it had already fallen in my spirit, and I was in the pit again. Now, however, I had hope, and that made all the difference.

"The following day the knowledge that someone cared for me gave me strength to face the day. I fed little Angelyn and put her down for her morning nap. This had usually been the worst time of my day. I was alone, and the baby didn't need me. Now, however, inspired by the worship service of the previous day and the pastor's prayers, I began to pray. As I paced back and forth through the house, I remembered the songs we had sung in church, and I began to sing them aloud, trying to recreate the worship atmosphere which had helped me so much. When I couldn't remember any more songs to sing, I prayed, asking God over and over to rescue me from the pit of depression.

"I did not experience immediate release, rather, an easing of symptoms, much like with any other illness. As I prayed and sang, worshiping God in the quiet of my house, the pain decreased. In this way, I endured the next two days, waiting for Wednesday night, when I could go to church again and be surrounded by the love and the presence of God that I had missed so much.

"Each morning during Angelyn's nap time, I read my Bible and prayed and sang the praise songs we were learning at church. I even made tapes of the music I loved. Peyton helped me edit them so I could have over an hour of praise and worship songs — because that was what seemed to help me the most.

"I listened to my worship tapes over and over. When feelings of depression began to rise up inside me, I could think about them and 'play' the tape in my mind. And, as the music filled my mind, depression could not overwhelm me.

"In the weeks that followed, I continued to worship God

Ground Level Christianity

daily, meeting Him every morning with praise songs, prayers and tears, but they were less and less often tears of sadness. As time passed and God healed my emotions, I more often had tears of joy at being in God's presence once again. I began to laugh some and to take a little interest in the house and in visiting my friends.

"Then one day, three months after Angelyn was born, I was driving our blue Chevrolet station wagon toward the west. Sunlight reflecting off the hood of the car directly into my eyes forced me to put down the visor, and suddenly, I realized it: The sun was shining! I looked around in shock. Such light! It was all so bright! I had not seen sunshine in three months. That, of course, wasn't possible. The sunlight had been there all along, but I just hadn't been able to see it because of the sadness I had been feeling.

"It was over now. I was out of the pit."

Kim gave herself freely to worship, and God tenderly met her need. It hurts me to admit that I was the "well-meaning, unfeeling" one who suggested that Kim might be experiencing a little "post-partum depression."

Kim learned what God wants us all to know: that He is our personal Father God who has designed worship as the way for us to experience Him. He seeks the true worshiper who will worship Him in Spirit and in truth — no façade, no lies, no superficiality. It touches the heart of God. In return, He pours out His love, joy and peace and His holy presence into our hearts. God is the only One who can meet our needs, and He has provided worship as a means for us to connect with Him.

Chapter 22

The Devil Made Me Do It

"Nobody seems to take the devil seriously like they did when I was growing up in the country," a young friend said recently. Although he was a "city boy," he had spent a lot of time with family members on their farm in the country. "They often talked about the devil — the part he played in the events of nature. They said the way some people acted could only be explained by a satanic power that hurt folks and messed up their lives." Now, with a few more years of experience in life, he added, "If people have ever been on drugs or alcohol, Satan will try to get them under his influence again. Folks in the country are more realistic about the devil. They know that the supernatural is real and that the devil won't let them alone."

A recovering alcoholic agrees. She says, "It takes more than human determination to stay free. It takes a life-transforming encounter with God. In Alcoholics Anonymous, the leaders plainly state that the new life comes from God. They talk about the Higher Power and say it in many different ways, but they are pretty open. They say 'You can change your behavior for a time (even a long time), but unless you have a real encounter with God, the old person will surface, and the behavior will reappear.'

"Even after you have new life in God through Jesus, the enemy will do whatever it takes to get you back. There is no room for complacency because we have everything to lose.

"But the ones I've seen stay clean are serious about their new life in Christ and their dependence on the Higher Power to keep them from falling back. It's so easy to fall back." She shook her head sadly, saying, "We just don't deal with the reality of the devil."

Ground Level Christianity
Belief in Reincarnation

Mike, a baby boomer, spoke about the way his contemporaries deal with the supernatural: "People in my generation who do talk about the hereafter or the supernatural, talk about reincarnation. The devil has sold them a lie they can be comfortable with. Reincarnation says they can come back to live a life better than the one they are messing up now. That way they don't have to deal with sin in their lives. They don't have to acknowledge that they need forgiveness, that only Jesus paid the sin price for us, that without blood sin can't be removed or forgiven. Reincarnation tells them that they'll have another chance to do a better job. They don't know that the Bible says that *'man is destined to die once, and after that to face judgment'* (Hebrews 9:27). People like to make up their own theology, I guess," Mike finished.

Drugs, alcohol and gambling are only some of the more conspicuous ways the devil seduces us. Less obvious are occult involvement,[1] such as reading one's horoscope, using a ouïji board, playing "fantasy games" like "Dungeons and Dragons," having a seance or levitating for fun. To most people these pastimes seem innocent enough. They dally with them without realizing that there are evil spirits behind all these activities.

Astrology and Horoscopes

"What sign are you?" a friend asked me at a party. I knew that being born in May put me under the sign of Taurus, the bull, but I wouldn't tell her, because that would draw me into a conversation I couldn't handle. "What's wrong with her reading her horoscope in the paper?" I asked God later.

After God reminded me of the scriptures in Deuteronomy, Leviticus, Isaiah[2] and others, He summarized: "If you look to any source other than your Heavenly Father for guidance or power, you have looked to the devil." Oh! Now I understood.

The Devil Made Me Do It

Most of us, at one time or another, have had our palms read, been exposed to tarot cards, even been to a hypnotist's show or a seance conducted by a professional. Any dealing with the supernatural that is not of God will open a door into our souls to the devil. He always enters at our invitation. He will stay there until an opportune time comes for him to enlarge his place, invite other evil spirits in to hurt us any way he can. Jesus said, *"The thief's purpose is to steal, kill and destroy"* (John 10:10, TLB).

The Remedy

Any occult involvement breaks the First Commandment, which prohibits putting any other gods before Almighty God.[3] It is sin, and we know what to do about sin. We confess it. We repent. We receive forgiveness by faith because Jesus paid the sin price on the cross. By faith we receive righteousness in the place of the unrighteousness, and we are clean.[4] No one can oust the devil from your soul better than you can and, thanks be to God, Jesus has given us the power to do just that.

Mike added, "Anyone who has been caught in the web of alcohol or drugs really knows what Peter meant when he wrote that the devil is like *"a roaring lion seeking whom he may devour"* (KJV).[5] Once the devil has a foothold in your life, he is hard to dislodge and even harder to keep away. He is very patient. He'll be there when your defenses are down. He knows just what will tempt you.

"Many churchgoing people don't take the devil seriously either, which is just what he wants. That way Satan can come up on their blind side, and they'll never know what hit them," Mike said with grim conviction.

The Existence of Witches

Another young man, David, would agree. David grew up on the mission field. "We could see that the devil was real

— to the missionaries as well as to the native people. I've seen the enemy display dramatic power, and that's when the Lord works in overwhelming ways."

Closer to home, he spoke about an experience with two witches in Virginia Beach, Virginia. "I lived near Regent University, a beautiful place to walk and jog. It was my custom to walk and pray God's blessings and authority over the area. Often, I would see two women doing the same thing, but in a hostile way. It became apparent to me that they were witches, casting spells, so I prayed more diligently. I'd seen this before as a child on the mission field.

"One evening I seemed called to go jogging — something unusual for me. As I jogged around, I proclaimed the lordship of Jesus Christ over the area and declared the power of God in that place. When I got close to the university, I saw the two women doing their thing, so I did mine. I spoke to the principalities and powers and wicked spirits in high places and, in the name of Jesus, brought them into obedience to Christ.[6] On my return trip, I saw the women again, but this time they were cowering behind a picket fence. After that, they never came back.

"Christians need to be aware that the devil attacks in subtle ways as well as overtly. We are ready for the punch, but we need to guard against the back hand," David said. "We need to pray for protection for the warriors and also for their family members and others who are close to them.

"After this Virginia Beach encounter, God seemed very distant from me. I felt a kind of spiritual numbness. I kept up Bible study and prayer, but I couldn't get rid of the wooden feeling in my life. Then one day in a prayer setting I took authority over that smothering spirit and the thing snapped. I was free. For the next four hours God reestablished our relationship and the vision for my life," David finished.

Both of these young men learned to use the spiritual weapons available to them so that they could prevail over Satan's attempts against their souls.

The Devil Made Me Do It
Guarding Our Thoughts and Deeds

One of the most valuable lessons I ever learned came from a college student, Ruth. In the academic arena, the struggle for the mind of the young people is intense. Which ideology will prevail? Ruth discovered that the battleground with Satan was her mind.[7] What provoked the battle? Thoughts. Sometimes it was loose talk among the students. Sometimes it was an accusation, a suspicion. Sometimes it was just glands that gave rise to unbidden thoughts. Behind those thoughts, however, Ruth concluded, the devil was working.

What Ruth learned is that our God helps us. He said, *"When the enemy shall come in like a flood, the Spirit of the LORD shall lift up a standard against him"* (Isaiah 59:19, KJV).

When something assailed her, Ruth learned to summon this answer: "I cast down this imagination! I cast out this thing that exalts itself against the knowledge of God! And I bring every thought into captivity to the obedience of Christ!" Describing her method of combating unwanted thoughts, she grabbed the side of her head as if to seize the vile thought and hurled it to the floor, an enactment of *"casting down imaginations"* (2 Corinthians 10:5, KJV).[8] In a moment, the thought was gone.

Socrates said that the thought is the father of the deed. The mind is the battleground for all of us. If Satan can insinuate an ungodly thought or suspicion or any untruth into our minds, he has half the battle won. *"He [Satan] is a liar and the father of lies,"* Jesus said (John 8:44). Satan's weapons are lies and fear.

Quickly, before a thought gives rise to a deed, we must bring all our thoughts into the obedience to Christ. Then Jesus is the honored one, Jesus is the victor, and we have not fathered a deed that will shame us and bring dishonor to His name.

This is what James and Peter meant when they warned us to resist the devil so that he will flee. We can take the devil seriously without seeing a demon under every bush. We choose whom we will obey, whom we will serve — just

Ground Level Christianity

like Adam did, just like Jesus did. Therefore the devil can't make me do it if I don't want to.

Endnotes: The Devil Made Me Do It

1. **Deuteronomy 18:10-13**—Let no one be found among you who sacrifices his son or daughter in the fire, who practices divination or sorcery, interprets omens, engages in witchcraft, or casts spells, or who is a medium or spiritist, or who consults the dead. Anyone who does these things is detestable to the LORD ... . You must be blameless before the LORD your God.
2. **Leviticus 20:27**—A man or woman who is a medium or a spiritist among you must be put to death ... their blood will be on their own heads. [This includes fortune-tellers, palm readers, Ouïja board operators, tarot card readers, tea leaves readers, crystal ball gazers, and readers of crystals (so popular now), horoscopes, and numerology. They all violate the first commandment and subvert the role of the Holy Spirit to lead us into all truth (John 16:13)].
Isaiah 8:19—So why are you trying to find out the future by consulting witches and mediums? Don't listen to their whisperings and mutterings. Can the living find out the future from the dead? Why not ask your God? (TLB).
3. **Exodus 20:2-3**—I am the LORD your God, who brought you out of Egypt, out of the land of slavery. Your shall have no other gods before me.
4. **1 John 1:9**—If we confess our sins, he [God] is faithful and just to forgive us our sins and to cleanse us from all unrighteousness (KJV).
5. **1 Peter 5:8**—Be self-controlled and alert. Your enemy the devil prowls around like a roaring lion looking for someone to devour.
6. **Ephesians 6:11-12**—Put on all of God's armor so that you will be able to stand safe against all the strategies and tricks of Satan. For we are not fighting against people made of flesh and blood, but against persons without bodies — the evil rulers of the unseen world, those mighty satanic beings and great evil princes of darkness who rule this world; and against huge numbers of wicked spirits in the spirit world (TLB).

The Devil Made Me Do It

7. **2 Corinthians 10:2-5**—... to those of you who persist in reckoning that our activities are on a purely human level. The truth is that, although we lead normal human lives, the battle we are fighting is on the spiritual level. The very weapons we use are not human but powerful in God's warfare for the destruction of the enemy's strongholds. Our battle is to break down every deceptive argument and every imposing defense that men erect against the true knowledge of God. We fight to capture every thought until it acknowledges the authority of Christ ... we are ready to punish every disobedience (PHIL).
8. **2 Corinthians 10:5**—Casting down imaginations, and every high thing that exalteth itself against the knowledge of God, and bringing into captivity every thought to the obedience of Christ (KJV).

Chapter 23

Choosing to Be Like Christ

"I believe we choose where we will be in eternity," Edna mused when we were gathered around the fireplace one wintry day for our prayer group. My ears pricked up. *Choose?* I glanced from the fire to her face to catch her words.

"Doesn't everybody who is born-again into the Kingdom of God in this life spend eternity with God?" Ann asked.

"Well, yes." Edna said. "That's the first choice: whether we'll spend eternity with God or the devil. Some people don't choose to make Jesus their Lord and to ask for forgiveness of sins, so they choose the devil by default. Many people, even church members, have never been born again of the Spirit of God."

That's the way I was, sitting in the church choir all those years before I became a Christian, I thought, while Edna continued.

"Jesus said, *'You must be born again or you cannot see the Kingdom of God,'* otherwise one goes to Hell[1] to be with devil and his fallen angels in everlasting punishment."[2]

"Go on," Ann prompted, because we already knew that.

"Then we choose whether we'll be in the Bride."

The Bride? I thought. *Isn't everyone in Heaven going to be in the Bride? Maybe not. Revelation tells of the marriage of Christ with His Church [Bride], and of those who are called to the Marriage Supper of the Lamb.*[3] *So maybe they are different,*

Edna had our attention as she continued. "It seems that in the Kingdom of Heaven, besides Jesus and His Bride, there will be others, too. John the Baptist called himself a friend of the Bridegroom in the story he told in John.[4] Jesus spoke of wise virgins who had oil in their lamps and foolish ones who let their oil run out and were outside when the door to the wedding feast was shut."[5]

Choosing to Be Like Christ

"What else?" Barbara asked for all of us. We were growing more anxious with every word.

"Remember the story Jesus told of the one who tried to come to the marriage of the king's son without the proper wedding garment? The king told his servants to bind him, take him away and cast him into outer darkness where there would be 'weeping and gnashing of teeth.' "[6]

"How much farther from the Bridegroom can you get!" exclaimed Mary. By now nobody was looking at the fire. We were looking into our hearts.

Just Barely in Heaven

"Well, some are just barely in Heaven at all. I know people who are born again. They are just as saved as they'll ever be, but salvation has made very little difference in their lives. I've wondered about that, and I believe it's because they've never made Jesus Lord of their lives.

"They don't have the power to live the Christian life, the power to share the Gospel and see people saved. They don't understand scripture for themselves, *'never able to come to the knowledge of the truth.'*[7] They'll go to Heaven but won't be enjoying Heaven on Earth in the meantime.

"Such things are not important to them until Jesus is truly Lord in their lives. Then they want to please Him, to be baptized in His Holy Spirit, to extend His Kingdom, to feed on His Word and to have the intimate relationship with Jesus described in the Song of Songs — here and eternally. When Jesus is our Lord, we want to be His Bride."

"I want to," said Mary. She spoke for all of us. "Tell us more."

The crackling fire was now in Edna, who was fueled by the Holy Spirit. "Do we ever consider why God saved us? Just to keep us from Hell? Just to take us to Heaven? Just to bring Heaven to Earth? All these are wonderful enough, but God had a bigger plan for us when He saved us. It was to make us like Jesus.[8] Why? So Jesus would have a Bride.

Ground Level Christianity
A Bride for Jesus

"Jesus is coming again to claim His Bride. In the meantime '... *we wait for the blessed hope — the glorious appearing of our great God and Savior, Jesus Christ, who gave himself for us to redeem us from all wickedness and to purify for himself a people that are his very own, eager to do what is good.*' I just read that today before I came," Edna said, "It's in Titus — 2:13 and 14."

"Doesn't it say in John somewhere that when Jesus appears we'll be like Him?" Barbara asked. Then, leafing through her Bible, she found the place and read: *"Dear Friends, now we are children of God, and what we will be has not yet been made known. But we know that when he appears, we shall be like him, for we shall see him as he is. Everyone who has this hope in him purifies himself, just as he is pure"* (1 John 3:2-3).

"I remember that Paul teaches somewhere that we become *'one flesh'* with Christ. He says it's *'a profound mystery,'*" Mary added.

A Profound Mystery

Ann always had her Bible and concordance handy. She found that scripture and read it to us: "... *just as Christ loved the church and gave himself up for her to make her holy, cleansing her by the washing with water through the word, and to present her to himself as a radiant church, without stain or wrinkle or any other blemish, but holy and blameless ... for we are members of his body ... and the two will become one flesh. This is a profound mystery — but I am talking about Christ and the church"* (Ephesians 5:25-27 and 30-32).

"Sometimes we might be tempted to 'spiritualize' this passage," Ann added. "We might want to avoid the issue that Christ wants that kind of closeness with His Body, the Church — you and me. But that is the plain statement of the Scriptures."

Edna took up the thread again. "God's plan is to make us

Choosing to Be Like Christ

like Jesus so He will have a Bride like Himself to make the 'Song of Songs' come true, so that He will have a Bride for total intimacy with Himself. Total union. Complete harmony. Listen to this ..." (she began to pick out descriptions from the Song of Songs): *"My lover is mine and I am his"* (2:16), *"All beautiful you are, my darling; there is no flaw in you"* (4:7), *"How much more pleasing is your love than wine"* (4:10), *"I belong to my lover, and his desire is for me"* (7:11), *"Come, my lover, let us go to the countryside ... there I will give you my love"* (7:10 and 12), *"Place me like a seal over your heart, like a seal on your arm; for love is as strong as death .... It burns like a blazing fire, like a mighty flame"* (8:6), *"I have become in his eyes like one bringing contentment"* (8:10).

"Did you know that Jesus loves us like that? No wonder He wants us to be in His Bride!

"The Bride is a mystery, yet it is a certainty," she continued. "The Marriage of the Lamb is the climax of all history — the reason for Creation, the reason for the atonement, for salvation, for going on to perfection. It's our *'blessed hope.'* "

"Oh, Edna," said Barbara, "now I see the reason for being born again. I mean, more than just because it's fire insurance. I see the reason for being baptized in the Holy Spirit. I mean, more than just the thrills and the power, and the reason for living a holy life. It's preparation for taking our place in Heaven with Jesus — in the place He's prepared for us."

"Yes," Edna replied, "but there's a lot more to this than we know. Some respected scholars say that every born-again believer will be in the Kingdom of Heaven and, therefore, will be in the Bride.

"That position relieves anyone of the responsibility of trying to sort out who's going to be in the Bride and who's not — or who is a wise or a foolish virgin. We're free to get on with our Christian lives — to *'seek first the kingdom of God and his righteousness, and all these things will be added unto you,'* "[9] she finished.

I've always been grateful to Edna for giving us the long view that day by the fire. We have an eternal goal to work toward. In the meantime, we are getting to know our Lord, becoming humble, bearing fruit for Jesus, learning to exercise the gifts of the Spirit, fasting, becoming transformed, cleaned up and healed, and we're bringing others into the Kingdom. We are becoming more and more like Jesus.

Once we get the concept of the Christian life as that of a Body — a Bride for Jesus — we realize how much we need one another. The Body is composed of members, all mutually interdependent and harmonious, each with a unique part to play and all necessary to the whole.[10] There is one Head for this Body — Jesus. He has promised to give us the mind of Christ[11] so we can move together in unity (see 1 Corinthians 12:12-28).

Worship Transforms

The more members of the Body of Christ we can meet with for worship, the better, for the whole is greater than the sum of all its parts. We come together in the joy of the heavenly hosts, who are always praising God and saying, *"Amen! Praise and glory and wisdom and thanks and honor and power and strength be to our God for ever and ever. Amen!"* (Revelation 7:12).

In the blending of our voices, our personalities, our enthusiasm and our wills in worshiping Almighty God and His Son, corporate worship takes on a dimension beyond the physical realm and puts us in touch, for the time, with the heavenly realm. When we come into the presence of God, He changes us. The Scriptures teach us that we shall not only behold Him, but we shall become like Him.

Jesus also says we will be with Him: *"I am not praying for these alone but also for the future believers who will come to me because of the testimony of these. My prayer for all of them is that they will be of one heart and mind, just as you and I are, Father — that just as you are in me and I am in you, so they will be in us, and the world will believe you sent me. I have given them the glory you gave me — the glorious unity of being one, as we are — I in them and you in me, all being perfected into one — so that the world will know you sent me and will understand that you love*

Choosing to Be Like Christ

them as much as you love me. Father, I want them with me — those you've given me — so that they can see my glory" (John 17:20-24, TLB).

So we are with Him now — or can be with Him now — and not just after we go to Heaven. This is so that the world will know that God sent Jesus to them, too. This is for us now — in worship with other believers with the same vision. In worship *"... we all, with open face beholding as in a glass the glory of the Lord, are changed into the same image from glory to glory, even as by the Spirit of the Lord"* (2 Corinthians 3:18, KJV).

It Is Supernatural

Supernatural? Of course. Nothing less would do justice to Almighty God. Nothing less could satisfy our deepest need to be freed from the shackles of self. Only a supernatural work can free us from sin for which Jesus had to come and die. And nothing less could allow us to live forever, together, with Him — free and transformed into His likeness.

God chose the blessed life for us — for you and me — in the beginning, in the Garden, and Jesus chooses this end for us when we truly become His Bride. The outcome, however, is our choice. Whether or where we will be with Jesus in Heaven is the fruit of our *Ground Level Christianity*.

Endnotes: Choosing to Be Like Christ

1. **John 3:16-20**—For God so loved the world that he gave his one and only Son, that whoever believes in him shall not perish but have eternal life. For God did not send his Son into the world to condemn the world, but to save the world through him. Whoever believes in him is not condemned, but whoever does not believe stands condemned already because he has not believed in the name of God's one and only Son. This is the verdict: Light has come into the world, but men loved darkness instead of light because their deeds were evil.
2. **Jude 14**: Enoch ... prophesied ... "See, the Lord is coming with

thousands upon thousands of his holy ones to judge everyone, and to convict all the ungodly of all the ungodly acts they have done in the ungodly way, and of all the harsh words ungodly sinners have spoken against him."

Jude 6-7—And the angels who did not keep their positions of authority but abandoned their own home — these he has kept in darkness, bound with everlasting chains for judgment on the great Day ... . They serve as an example of those who suffer the punishment of eternal fire.

3. **Revelation 19:7 and 9**—Let us rejoice and be glad and give him glory! For the wedding of the Lamb has come, and his bride has made herself ready ... . Then the angel said to me, "Write: 'Blessed are those who are invited to the wedding supper of the Lamb!'"

4. **John 3:29**—The bride belongs to the bridegroom. The friend who attends the bridegroom waits and listens for him, and is full of joy when he hears the bridegroom's voice. That joy is mine, and it is now complete.

5. In **Matthew 25:1-12**, Jesus tells this story:

    "At that time the kingdom of heaven will be like ten virgins who took their lamps and went out to meet the bridegroom. Five of them were foolish and five were wise. The foolish ones took their lamps but didn't take any oil with them. The wise, however, took oil in jars along with their lamps. The bridegroom was a long time in coming, and they all became drowsy and fell asleep.

    "At midnight the cry rang out: 'Here's the bridegroom! Come out to meet him!'

    "Then all the virgins woke up and trimmed their lamps. The foolish ones said to the wise, 'Give us some of your oil; our lamps are going out.'

    " 'No,' they replied, 'there may not be enough for both us and you. Instead, go to those who sell oil and buy some for yourselves.'

    "But when they were on their way to buy the oil, the bridegroom arrived. The virgins who were ready went in with him to the wedding banquet. And the door was shut.

    "Later the others also came. 'Sir, Sir!' they said. 'Open the door for us!'

Choosing to Be Like Christ

"But he replied, 'I tell you the truth, I don't know you,'
"Therefore keep watch, because you don't know the day or the hour."

6. Jesus tells another story in **Matthew 22:1-12**:

   "The kingdom of heaven is like a king who prepared a wedding banquet for his son ... . Then he said to his servants. 'The banquet is ready, but those I have invited did not deserve to come. Go to the street corners and invite anyone you find.' So the servants went out to the streets and gathered all the people they could find, both good and bad, and the wedding hall was filled with guests.

   "But when the king came in to see the guests, he noticed a man there who was not wearing wedding clothes. 'Friend,' he asked, 'how did you get in here without wedding clothes?' The man was speechless.

   "Then the king told the attendants, 'Tie him hand and foot, and throw him outside, into the darkness, where there will be weeping and gnashing of teeth.'

   "For many are invited, but few are chosen."

7. **2 Timothy 3:7**—... always learning and never able to come to the knowledge of the truth (KJV).

8. **2 Corinthians 3:18**—And we, who with unveiled faces all reflect the Lord's glory, are being transformed into his likeness with ever-increasing glory, which comes from the Lord who is the Spirit.

9. **Matthew 6:33**—Jesus is bringing the Sermon on the Mount to a conclusion, saying:

   "But seek first his kingdom and his righteousness, and all these things will be given to you as well."

10. In **1 Corinthians 12:12-28**, Paul explains the organic whole of the Body of Christ made up of individual members.

11. **1 Corinthians 2:16**—But we have the mind of Christ.

The Last Word

Is it possible that you, dear reader, have not settled your eternal life (destiny) with Jesus? Have you ever prayed and asked Jesus to forgive your sins and receive you as His child? If you haven't done this as a mature person who is responsible for an adult commitment, and you really don't know whether you'll go to Heaven when you die, you can settle the matter before you close this book. Take these simple steps:

1. Acknowledge that God is your Maker, and Jesus is His Son, Who died on the cross to pay the price of redemption for all people everywhere.

2. Acknowledge that God raised Jesus from the dead, and that He lives forever in a resurrected body. God did this to provide resurrection life for everyone who receives Jesus as Lord by faith. Resurrection life begins with this confession and lasts through death for eternity with Father God and all His saints.

3. Acknowledge that you have sinned and that you need forgiveness and a new life.

4. Say something like Dreama did, or Penny did, or David did. Pray out loud to Jesus.

5. Be sure to tell someone about your decision. If you like, fill out the statement on the following page and send it to me. I'll pray with you and for you.

I, _____, believe that Jesus died on the cross for my sins. I believe that God raised Jesus from the dead to provide resurrection life for me as I take Jesus to be my Savior and Lord.

I ask You, Jesus, to be my Lord and forgive my sins. I repent of my sins and ask You to be my Savior. Please accept me as Your child forever, and give me a new life with You. By faith I receive forgiveness and eternal life.

Date_____

To send me your statement of commitment to Christ, my address is:

Janice Gravely
540 Falls Road
Rocky Mount, NC 27804

Call for prayer on this or any other need:
Telephone (252) 446-4320 (Eastern Standard Time)

Appendix

A Brief Sketch of the Bible

For those who are new to the Bible, allow me to give you a brief overview of it:

As a narrative, the Bible is a thriller. It starts off with a bang. God created the whole universe out of NOTHING by His creative Word. He said, *"Let there be light,"* and *"there was light!"* (Genesis 1:3, KJV). He called the light Day, and the darkness He called Night. He made the heavens around the Earth to carry moisture, and divided the waters on the Earth from the dry land. Then He commanded the ground to bring forth grass and trees bearing fruit, and He saw that it was good. Next God commanded lights in the heaven to divide day from night, so they would be *"for signs and seasons, and for days and years"* (Genesis 1:14, NKJ). God spoke into existence fish and fowl of every kind, then beasts and cattle, and God saw that it was good.

The perfect creation's beginning and the corruption of it all take only a few hundred words to describe. The stage was set. Then God created man: *"Then God said, 'Let us make man in our image, in our likeness, and let them rule over the fish of the sea and the birds of the air, over the livestock, over all the earth ... .' So God created man in his own image ... male and female he created them"* (Genesis 1:26-27).

All of this He did with the creative power of His Word!

Created to Love

God did all this so He could have someone like Himself to connect with and love — the perfect pair, Adam and Eve. God presented the Earth to Adam and Eve and gave them dominion, the rule over it all. He summoned all the animals to Adam for him to name. Imagine thinking up a different name for every animal in the world! Hippopotamus, giraffe, cow, rhinoceros, orangutan, ostrich, fox ... . For brilliant Adam it was easy because he had no limitations. By the act of naming the animals, Adam exerted lordship over them. He exercised the privilege of dominion.

Ground Level Christianity

Like God, Adam also had the creative word in his mouth. Like God, Adam had free will. Like Adam, we today are made in the image and likeness of God, with free will and the creative word in our mouths.

God and His children, Adam and Eve, had sweet communion and perfect fellowship with God ... until Adam exercised his free will when he chose to obey Satan's invitation to eat the forbidden fruit. In this one act Adam chose Satan over God, and the consequences were fatal. Sin entered the world because disobedience is sin, and with sin came death, because *"the soul who sins shall die"* (Ezekiel 18:4, NKJ). Furthermore, when Adam transferred his loyalty to Satan, the dominion God had given to Adam over all the Earth went with it. Poof! Satan became the *"god of this world"* (2 Corinthians 4:4, NAS).

Banished from God's Garden

After they disobeyed God, Adam and Eve were expelled from Paradise. They came under the cruel taskmaster, Satan, because *"you are slaves to the one whom you obey,"* Paul says in Romans 6:16. Whereas they had tended the garden, now they rooted out thorns and thistles by the sweat of Adam's brow, and Eve brought forth children in hard labor. Even then, God promised a Redeemer to spring forth from her seed (see Genesis 3:15). The nature of sin caused one of her sons to murder the other (Cain and Abel), but the godly line was reestablished in Seth.

Ungodliness prevailed until God regretted ever having made man at all. But He looked until He found a man who would listen and obey Him -- Noah. Up to this time, moisture had stayed up in the heavens and drenched the Earth with dew every night, so nobody had ever heard of rain, and certainly not floods. Even so, Noah obeyed God, and for years he labored to build an ark that would float on nonexistent water from nonexistent rain. At God's word, Noah brought into the ark his wife, his three sons and their wives, and pairs of animals of every species. Then the rains came, and waters were released from the deeps. After forty days and nights of rain, all creation was destroyed except the life that was preserved on the ark.

Just as God had promised Adam and Eve a Redeemer, He promised Noah that the world would never again be destroyed by floods, and He put a rainbow in the sky as a sign of the covenant

Appendix

promise. In this covenant, God also ordained human government to keep civil order among the people who would spring forth from Noah's sons — a temporary caretaker until Jesus returns to rule the world.

From Noah's sons, Shem, Ham and Japheth, the world was repopulated and organized into nations with governments. All this was under the lordship of Satan, who still holds the dominion surrendered by Adam.

Again people became wicked and corrupt. In that wicked world God still looked for a man to believe Him and obey Him. He found Abram in Ur of the Chaldees.

Abraham — God's Man

When Abram was seventy-five years old, God appeared to him and told him to go to a distant land where He would make of him a great nation, as numerous as the stars in the sky. Although Abram and his wife Sarai had no children, God said to them, *"I will bless those who bless you, and whoever curses you will I curse; and all peoples on earth will be blessed through you"* (Genesis 12:3), continuing his promise of blessing to Eve, another covenant. This time God "cut a covenant" with Abram. In the ancient world, as in some primitive societies still today, people made lasting vows to each other by exchanging cuts on the wrists, making them "blood brothers." Since God is Spirit (without blood), He used the blood of animals as a substitute. With the covenant, God changed Abram's name to Abraham, adding the H from His own name JHWH. With Sarai He did the same, and we know her now as Sarah. When the two of them accepted God as their Lord, He gave them a new name, just like Adam did with the animals.

A Godly Line

Abraham was one hundred years old and Sarah was ninety when their son Isaac was born. Isaac, who married Rebecca, a close relative, had twin sons, Esau and Jacob. Jacob carried on the godly heritage begun by Abraham and Isaac. Esau, sadly, never valued a relationship with God. Jacob had twelve famous, quarreling sons, who sired the twelve tribes of Israel.

How did they get to Egypt? Of Jacob's twelve sons, Rachel's son Joseph was the favorite. Joseph had dreams that eleven shocks of wheat and eleven stars bowed down to him. When he told the dreams to his brothers, in a jealous rage they planned to kill him. Instead they put him in a dry cistern until Midianite merchants came along. The brothers sold Joseph to these merchants, and the merchants, in turn, took him to Egypt to sell him into slavery.

As a slave, Joseph learned to trust God in everything. He interpreted Pharaoh's dream foretelling famine in the world, saying, *"It is not in me: God shall give Pharaoh an answer of peace"* (Genesis 41:16, KJV). Pharaoh rewarded Joseph's wisdom with the second highest place in his kingdom.

It was famine that drove Jacob and his family of sixty-six to Egypt, where Joseph, now in charge of the distribution of scarce grains, gave them food and the best pasture lands, a place known as Goshen. There the Hebrews lived to themselves for the next four hundred years, herding sheep and cattle until they had grown so numerous that the Egyptians became afraid of them and enslaved them.

Now God had a people, a nation, to carry out the covenants and to live out the scriptures.

Moses, the Plagues, the Red Sea, the Desert and the Trip Back to the Promised Land

Enter Moses. He was born four hundred years after Joseph, when a different pharaoh feared that the enslaved Hebrews would outnumber the Egyptians and decreed the death of all the Hebrew baby boys. But Moses' mother hid him in the bulrushes until Pharaoh's daughter found him. She, having no children of her own, adopted him. Educated at court to be a royal prince, Moses sided with his Jewish heritage over his Egyptian inheritance, killed an Egyptian taskmaster, and then fled to the land of Midian where he married and tended sheep for his father-in-law for the next forty years.

Moses was eighty years old when God spoke to him from a burning bush and called him into service. Like Joseph, hard circumstances had crushed his pride and left him a humble man. He had lived as a prince and as a pauper. With education tempered by experience, Moses was a man equipped for service. God sent him back to Egypt to liberate about three million people. At Moses' command the Red Sea parted to let the multitude pass safely through on dry ground, and at his word the sea engulfed Pharaoh's

Appendix

mighty army. Moses led the Children of Israel through desert wilderness for forty years during which *"their clothes did not wear out nor did their feet become swollen"* (Nehemiah 9:21).

The finger of God chiseled out the Ten Commandments on stone tablets for Moses to give to the Israelites. Those laws and the special relationship God had with Abraham's offspring set Jews apart from all other people in the ancient (and even the modern) world.

Most scholars agree that Moses wrote the first five books of the Bible, which record miracles and fascinating stories, but chiefly they reveal a God who is longsuffering and of great mercy, easily entreated, and keeper of His covenants.

Moses died in the wilderness, leaving this message with his people: *"Blessed are you, O Israel! Who is like you, a people saved by the Lord? He is your shield and helper and your glorious sword. Your enemies will cower before you, and you will trample down their high places"* (Deuteronomy 33:29).

Conquering the Promised Land

Of the original three million people who left Egypt, only Joshua and Caleb survived in leadership after forty years in the wilderness. Joshua (in the Book of Joshua) succeeded Moses and brought the nation of Israel across the Jordan River. The Jordan parted at flood tide, just as the Red Sea had parted for Moses. During Joshua's lifetime the children of Israel conquered most of the Promised Land (the land of Canaan, promised to Abraham and his descendants) and lived under the Law given by God through Moses.

Spiritual and military leaders, called judges, succeeded Joshua in leading, for more than three hundred years, a people who sometimes obeyed the God of Abraham. At other times they adopted the idolatry and evil ways of their neighbors. The Book of Judges recounts the cycles of obedience (associated with material blessing and military success) and disobedience (associated with poverty and military oppression). Finally the Israelites cried out for a king to lead them so that they could be like other nations. Despite warnings from the prophet Samuel that such a human ruler could never govern as well as God had governed His people, the people persisted in their desire, and God eventually relented and gave them a king.

Ground Level Christianity
Kings Saul, David and Solomon

God appointed an extraordinarily impressive young man named Saul to be the first king of Israel, confirming him by supernatural events. In Saul, however, we see that even an extraordinary man with an extraordinary beginning can end up a raging enemy of the God who anointed him. No Shakespearean play has more intrigue, ambition, triumph or disaster than the story of King Saul (see 1 Samuel).

Saul's successor was the famous King David, a young shepherd who defeated the nine-foot-tall Goliath with a sling and a stone. Like Joseph and Moses, David learned humility through hard experiences. Even when he had become a seasoned, cunning warrior, he would pray about battle strategies. At night he sang poetry to God, and early morning often found him worshiping the God who gave him victory.

But even David was not perfect. His moral failure with Bathsheba inspired this profound prayer for forgiveness: *"Have mercy on me, O God, according to your unfailing love; according to your great compassion blot out my transgressions ... . For I know my transgressions, and my sin is always before me. Against you, you only, have I sinned and done what is evil in your sight, so that you are proved right when you speak and justified when you judge ... . Surely you desire truth in the inner parts ... . Create in me a pure heart, O God, and renew a steadfast spirit within me"* (Psalm 51:1, 3-4, 6 and 10)

David's son Solomon, who was known for his wisdom and the magnificence of his kingdom, succeeded him. Solomon's reign was the golden age of Israel. He started out by asking God for wisdom to rule rather than for wealth or long life. God answered by giving him the greatest wealth the world has ever known, in addition to the wisdom he desired.

Solomon built the Temple for Almighty God, carrying out his father's plans and instructions. But Solomon was not tempered in the furnace of affliction like Noah, Joseph, Moses and David. Despite his success, Solomon's life turned into tragedy. He failed to follow God's commands. He married foreign wives and adopted the worship of their gods. Contrary to the Law of Moses, Solomon bought many chariots and war-horses, and his heart turned away from Jehovah.

You can hear Solomon's melancholy disillusionment in these lines from Ecclesiastes, which he wrote: *"I denied myself nothing*

Appendix

my eyes desired; I refused my heart no pleasure. My heart took delight in all my work, and this was the reward for all my labor. Yet when I surveyed all that my hands had done and what I had toiled to achieve, everything was meaningless, a chasing after the wind; nothing was gained under the sun" (Ecclesiastes 2:10-11).

Solomon was not the first nor the last man to begin well and end poorly. He wrote a thousand proverbs to help us end well, although he did not follow his own advice.

Solomon's son, Rehoboam, unwisely precipitated the rebellion of the ten northern tribes of Israel, leaving only two tribes, Judah and Benjamin, under his rule.

David's Kingdom Divides

While Rehoboam, king of Judah (as the Southern Kingdom was called), was not especially godly, the Northern Kingdom under Jeroboam went into total defiance of God. Jeroboam created golden calves for gods instead of worshipping in Solomon's Temple with the people of God.

For the next two hundred years, God sent prophets, like Elijah and Amos, to bring the Northern Kingdom back to the one true God. The Northern Kingdom quickly went from religious rebellion into lurid sexual practices and ritual infant murder.

Finally God allowed Israel to be conquered by Assyria and to be deported to that land. In exchange, Assyrians were resettled in Samaria. The Assyrians intermarried with the Jews who remained there and produced offspring who, in Jesus' time, were known and despised as Samaritans.

The four books of Kings and Chronicles track Judah and Israel from two different perspectives. For the most part, First and Second Kings are historical, and First and Second Chronicles are spiritual accounts of the same history. Isaiah and Jeremiah were the leading prophets in Judah.

About a hundred and eighty years after the deportation of Israel, Judah was conquered by Nebuchadnezzar, king of Babylon. The Babylonian army burned Solomon's Temple, destroyed the palaces and broke down the walls of Jerusalem. They took the Temple treasures to Babylon and killed most of the remaining people of Jerusalem.

The long history of God's people is covered in a little more than half of the Old Testament. The story begins in the five Books of

Ground Level Christianity

Moses, Joshua, Judges and Ruth. First and Second Samuel contain the account of Kings Saul and David. These two books were written, at least in part, by the judge Samuel and named for him. First and Second Kings and First and Second Chronicles complete the history of Israel and Judah until the land was conquered and the people deported. Then God stirred up the exiled Jews to return to Jerusalem and rebuild the Temple of the Most High God under the priest, Ezra, and to rebuild the walls of Jerusalem under the governor, Nehemiah. These accounts are found in books with those names.

Meanwhile, back in Babylon, where most of the Jews remained, ancient enemies of the Jews plotted to have every Jew in King Xerxes' empire (then all the known world) killed on a certain day. Queen Esther, a Jewess, risked her life to nullify the edict, being told by her uncle, Mordecai, that it was for such a time as this that she had come into the kingdom (see Esther 4:14). Her story is Another thriller.

The Poetical Books

The poetical books of the Bible are grouped together — Job, Psalms, Proverbs, Ecclesiastes and Song of Solomon. Most of the Psalms are attributed to David, and Solomon authored most of the Proverbs and the Song of Songs.

The psalms refresh, console, encourage, revitalize or identify a need of the moment. They teach us how to worship and how to pray. For example, even when terrible events of inner struggles are the subjects of a psalm, they are followed by expressions of praise and gratitude and by affirmations of God's goodness and His control over events.

Wise Solomon saved me one day when my husband and I were in Stuttgart, Germany. It was my birthday. For two hours I waited alone in a rented Mercedes in the parking lot of a little glider port in the fog while Edmund was "hangar flying" with the world champion soaring pilot. Neither of us spoke German, so for me it would be no better inside than out. I felt neglected and nursed my self-pity until I got mad.

Solomon to the rescue! He admonished me from the open Bible in my lap: *"The wise woman builds her house, but with her hands the foolish one tears hers down"* (Proverbs 14:1). Suddenly I knew I could

Appendix

bring mine down with my mouth because across the page it said, *"He who guards his lips guards his life, but he who speaks rashly will come to ruin"* (Proverbs 13:3).

I turned to Romans 6:14 which says, *"Sin shall not have dominion over you"* (KJV). As I confessed the sin of anger, I got free of it. When my husband came out, it was to a soft-spoken wife, and we drove happily off to Paris, where we celebrated my birthday and Mother's Day at the Ritz in Paris, France — thanks to connecting with the living Word of God.

As I said, the Book is alive.

The Prophets
Isaiah, Jeremiah and Ezekiel

The last portion of the Old Testament contains the writing of the Prophets, beginning with Isaiah and ending with Malachi. They are not arranged chronologically, but roughly from the longest to the shortest. In Isaiah and Jeremiah, Daniel and Ezekiel, we get many rich details of their times and the miracles they performed. In Isaiah we hear God reaching out to connect with His people when He says, " *'Come now, and let us reason together,' says the* LORD. *'Though your sins are like scarlet, they shall be as white as snow; though they are red as crimson, they shall be like wool. If you are willing and obedient, you will eat the best from the land; but if you resist and rebel, you shall be devoured with the sword: For the mouth of the* LORD *has spoken'* " (Isaiah 1:18-20).

Much of Handel's "Messiah" was taken from Isaiah. In Isaiah 53 the prophet described exactly the historical details of Jesus' death on the cross and what it would mean to future generations. Jesus quoted Isaiah 61:1-2 as His commission to minister in power, recorded in Luke 4. Several people I know have received this scripture as a personal mandate from God to go into the ministry. You may take it, too.

It says, *"The Spirit of the Sovereign* LORD *is on me, because the* LORD *has anointed me to preach good news to the poor. He has sent me to bind up the broken hearted, to proclaim freedom for the captives, and release from darkness for the prisoners, to proclaim the year of the* LORD's *favor ..."* (Isaiah 61:1-2).

Jeremiah was perhaps the most personal of the prophets because he spoke about human suffering, with hope and victory in

Ground Level Christianity

the midst of it because of God's faithfulness. He even gives us God's telephone number, and God's line is never busy. The number to call is Jeremiah 33:3. This verse says: *"Call to me and I will answer you and tell you great and unsearchable things you do not know."*

It is Jeremiah who tells of the New Covenant which will be made with Jesus' blood: *" 'The time is coming,' declares the LORD, 'when I will make a new covenant with the house of Israel and with the house of Judah ... . I will put my law in their minds and write it on their hearts. I will be their God and they will be my people ... . For I will forgive their wickedness and will remember their sins no more' "* (Jeremiah 31:31-34).

To learn what happened to the Jews in captivity we go to the prophets Ezekiel and Daniel. Ezekiel saw the glory of the Lord depart from the Temple of God in Jerusalem because of the corruption of the priests and kings and people. And he, too, foresaw that God's grace in the future would change mankind from the heart first: *"I will give them an undivided heart and put a new spirit in them; I will remove from them their heart of stone and give them a heart of flesh. Then they will follow my decrees and be careful to keep my laws. They will be my people and I will be their God"* (Ezekiel 11:19-20).

What is this new heart Jeremiah and Ezekiel prophesied for God's people? It is what the Bible calls a mystery. A Bible mystery is not like a Sherlock Holmes mystery. Rather it is something hidden waiting to be revealed at the proper time. The proper time to disclose this mystery came when Paul wrote to the Colossian church: *"I have become its [the church's] servant by the commission God gave me to present to you the word of God in its fullness — the mystery that has been kept hidden for ages and generations, but is now disclosed to the saints. To them God has chosen to make known among the Gentiles the glorious riches of this mystery, which is Christ in you, the hope of glory"* (Colossians 1:25-27).

"Christ in you" is the new heart, the *"heart of flesh"* replacing the stony heart that Ezekiel so accurately describes. Jesus actually comes into the heart of the born-again person and lives His life through the believer.

"Christ in you" IS a mystery which, once revealed to the heart and mind of the believer, brings understanding and unlocks all the other mysteries. The new heart allows the Christian life with all of its promises and possibilities to make sense and become reality.

Paul wrote further: *"My purpose is that they [the believers] may be*

Appendix

encouraged in heart and united in love, so that they may have the full riches of complete understanding, in order that they may know the mystery of God, namely Christ, in whom are hidden all the treasures of wisdom and knowledge" (Colossians 2:2-3).

What Jeremiah and Ezekiel foretold a millennium before, Paul revealed to us so we can both have Jesus in our hearts and show Him to the world.

Daniel

The book written by Daniel is another thriller. He was one of the princes brought as a Jewish captive into the royal court of Babylon after the fall of Jerusalem to be trained in Chaldean wisdom, knowledge, language and culture. The Chaldeans changed the names of Daniel's three Hebrew friends to Shadrach, Meshach and Abed-nego, and Daniel was renamed Belteshazzar. These four were offered the sumptuous food of the king but pleaded, instead, to be allowed to follow Jewish dietary and worship regulations. It was an early test of their faith and integrity, and they became more outstanding than all the other trainees — *"ten times better than all the magicians and astrologers that were in his [the king's] realm"* (Daniel 1:20).

When King Nebuchadnezzar, for example, had a frightening dream, he demanded that the wise men tell him the dream and the interpretation — on penalty of death. Only Daniel was able to do it. He said, *"There is a God in heaven who reveals mysteries. He has shown King Nebuchadnezzar what will happen in days to come"* (Daniel: 2:28-30). (Doesn't that sound like Joseph?) Daniel then told the king his dream: it was of a huge statue with head of gold, torso of silver, thighs of brass, legs of iron and feet part of iron and part of clay.

He also received the interpretation of the dream. Part of it was as follows: *"You saw a stone that was cut without hands smite the image on its feet of iron and clay and break them to pieces. Then the iron, the clay, the brass, the silver and the gold broke to pieces together, became like chaff and the wind blew them away. The stone that smote the image became a great mountain and filled the whole earth ... . You, O king, are a king of kings for the God of heaven has given your kingdom, power, and strength and glory ... . You are the head of gold ..."* (Daniel 2:31-38, my paraphrase).

Ground Level Christianity

History has born out this interpretation, and all that remains to be fulfilled is the *"stone filling the whole earth."* Can you guess who that *"stone"* is?

Because God had made King Nebuchadnezzar ruler over the known world, he was filled with pride and required that everyone worship a golden image that he had set up. A burning, fiery furnace was prepared for those who would not bow down when the music played. Shadrach, Meshach and Abed-nego refused, because if there was one thing the Jews learned from their overthrow in Jerusalem, it was NEVER to worship idols again. Called to account for their behavior, they said: *"... the God we serve is able to save us from it, and he will rescue us from your hand, O king. But even if he does not, we want you to know, O king, that we will not serve your gods or worship the image of gold you have set up"* (Daniel 3:17-18). So they were thrown into a furnace so hot it killed the men who cast them in. But you must read this for yourself; the writing is so colorful, so poetic, and so powerful. You will enjoy it.

Under a new king, Belshazzar, Daniel was called upon to interpret the handwriting on the wall. God's finger wrote of Belshazzar's defeat at the hand of Darius the Mede that very night.

Another time, Daniel's enemies tricked King Darius into outlawing Daniel's worship of God. Daniel responded by praying outloud near an open window every day. The king (also called Xerxes in the history books) trapped by his own edict, was forced to throw Daniel into the famous lion's den. Daniel's God kept him safe all night. When Darius discovered Daniel unhurt, he ordered the plotters to be thrown into the pit, where the lions devoured them before they touched the ground. As a result, Darius ordered that no other god should be worshiped in his kingdom except the God of Daniel.

The rest of the book contains Daniel's visions which predict history, and most of them have come to pass already. Some of Daniel's prophecies closely parallel the New Testament book of the Revelation.

The Minor Prophets

The rest of the prophets were active during the times of the kings of Israel and Judah and exhorted God's people to follow the one true God. Three prophets, Haggai, Zechariah and Malachi, however, encouraged the people of Ezra's and Nehemiah's day

Appendix

— the time when many Jews were returning from exile to live in Jerusalem and other portions of the Southern Kingdom. Not all Jews returned. Many stayed in Babylonia.

The Old Testament closes with Malachi, who foretold in a few words the ministry of John and Jesus: " *'See, I will send my messenger, who will prepare the way before me. Then suddenly the LORD you are seeking will come to his temple; the messenger of the covenant whom you desire will come,' says the LORD Almighty*" (Malachi 3:1).

Among the concluding words of the Old Testament are these: *"See, I will send you the prophet Elijah before that great and dreadful day of the LORD comes. He will turn the hearts of the fathers to their children, and the hearts of the children to their fathers; or else I will come and strike the land with a curse"* (Malachi 4:5-6).

The Gospels

The New Testament opens with names — all the names in the genealogy of Christ, crossing the chasm of four hundred silent years between the two testaments, linking Jesus with Father Abraham, Noah, Adam and God.

The four Gospel writers, Matthew, Mark, Luke and John, present different pictures of this God-man, but all are harmonious and complementary. By Jesus' life, death and resurrection they paint the heart of God spilled out in the ultimate sacrifice to bring sinful people to Himself in perfect love and communion. By His Holy Spirit, God finds a way to connect with people by living inside of us — in the new heart spoken of by Jeremiah and Ezekiel. Forever. Eternally.

Will we connect with God? Some will, some won't. It was the same in Jesus' day. Those who followed Jesus learned of Him and obeyed Him, and their lives were completely changed.

"Gospel" is a word meaning "good news," and is used for the four accounts, as well as for the message of salvation itself.

One event that is crucial in all four gospels is the death and resurrection of Jesus. This is the most well-documented event in history, included in secular as well as sacred reports. Belief in the resurrection is central to the Christian faith.

The History of the Church

Following the four gospels is the Book of Acts, the story of the birth of the early Church in Israel and other parts of the world. Churches came into being as people became followers of Jesus and banded together to worship the risen Lord.

Acts describes the world being *"turned upside down"* (as one observer put it) by the disciples and others who responded to the Gospel message and spread the Good News throughout the Roman Empire.

Saul (later known as Paul) became one of those messengers. Like Moses, he was brilliant and highly educated. Raised a strictly religious Jew, he zealously protected the Jewish faith, even to the point of killing and imprisoning Christians. On a Christian-persecution mission to the town of Damascus, Saul was struck down, blinded and commanded by Jesus to go to the house of a Christian believer in that city. There in Damascus, a Christian named Ananias prayed for Saul to receive the Holy Spirit and to recover his sight.

After his encounter with the Risen Christ, Saul changed completely, even changing his name to Paul. At the risk of his life, Paul immediately began preaching that Jesus is the Messiah, first to the Jews, and then to the Gentiles. The Book of Acts tells a great deal about what Paul did and endured for this faith. These stories are every bit as exciting as those of Daniel's life.

The Epistles

Paul's letter to the Romans follows the Book of Acts. It is first among the epistles ("epistle" just means "letter"), but it was written after a lifetime of teaching and preaching. It explains the theology of Christianity to both Jews and non-Jews.

New believers need instruction in what it means to be a Christian. Paul taught the Gentiles to receive the love of God and to shed their idols and immoralities. To the Jews he gave understanding of the new heart with the Law written within. Jews and Gentiles, then and now, need to understand that we are justified by faith alone. Other letters address thorny problems or particular needs.

In addition to Paul's letters, the New Testament includes letters from James (a half-brother of Jesus), Peter, John and Jude (also a half-brother of Jesus). It is not known for sure who wrote the letter to the Hebrews.

Appendix
The Climax of the Ages

The Bible closes with the Revelation of Jesus Christ to the Apostle John. As punishment for his faith and preaching, John was exiled to the Isle of Patmos. There he received from Jesus exhortations for first- and second-generation churches. Visions of the New Heaven and the New Earth came to him while he was worshiping alone on the Island of Patmos.

His book may be difficult to understand, but it is also the only book with this promise: *"Blessed is the one who reads the words of this prophecy, and blessed are those who hear it and take to heart what is written in it, because the time is near"* (Revelation 1:3).

Parts of the Revelation remind us of the prophecies in Isaiah, Ezekiel and Daniel. We see in it the declaration of God's victory over all evil, dire predictions of the end of time and the reward of those who are faithful to Jesus Christ.

Revelation concludes with a description of a *"new heaven and a new earth"* — a totally new creation — and those whose names are written in the Lamb's Book of Life may enter there.

In the last chapter of Revelation, Jesus says to everyone, *"Blessed are those who wash their robes, that they may have the right to the tree of life .... I am coming soon"* (Revelation 22:14 and 20).

The Bible is more than a good book you can curl up with for a wonderful afternoon. It is a book we can curl up in the lap of God with and hear His heartbeat until our hearts beat with His. We can be transformed into all that God enables us to be.

The whole world acknowledges the chronology of the Bible. Everything "before Christ" is counted backwards from the birth of Jesus, as in B.C., and everything since Jesus' birth is called A.D., standing for Anno Domini, Latin for "the year of our Lord." Whether they know it or not, people all over the world bow to the dominion of the Lord Jesus Christ and the God of the Bible.

Another great book by Janice Gravely:

Won't Somebody Help Me!

The story of a miracle attested to by *Reader's Digest,* Paul Harvey, *Guideposts* and "The 700 Club." Trapped in a light aircraft at 6,000 feet above the earth, her husband slumped unconscious in the pilot's seat beside her ...

Read the exciting account of how God saved Janice Gravely's life and helped her pilot the plane to safety, without having had any previous flying experience.

For your copy, or for additional copies of this book, send $10.00 each, plus $2.00 for postage to:

Janice Gravely
540 Falls Road
Rocky Mount, NC 27804